A Teacher of the Church

A Teacher of the Church
Theology, Formation, and Practice
for the Ministry of Teaching

Edited by Russ Moulds

Contributors:
Charles Blanco, Richard Carter,
Jane Fryar, Kenneth Heinitz,
W. Theophil Janzow, Russ Moulds,
James H. Pragman

Wipf & Stock
PUBLISHERS
Eugene, Oregon

A TEACHER OF THE CHURCH
Theology, Formation, and Practice for the Ministry of Teaching

ISBN 10: 1-55635-089-9
ISBN 13: 978-1-55635-089-4

Manufactured in the U.S.A.

"Nicodemus said to him, 'How can this be?'
Jesus answered him, 'Are you a teacher of Israel,
and yet you do not understand this?'"

John 3:9–10

Contents

Contents

Preface

WHEN IT comes to being and "doing" the Christian church, what counts? Far and away, two factors distinguish the effective spiritual growth and outreach of Christian fellowship.

The first is a friendly, welcoming community. This doesn't mean a lot of glad-handing, back-slapping, and trying too hard. It means at least a sizeable minority of folks—whether in the building, the sanctuary, the activities, the small groups, the staff, or the classes—who convey to others that the doors are open and this is a good place to be. The pastor and sermons do count, and, for better or worse, the first measure of a congregation is its pastor. Similarly, the Christian school community is characterized by the disposition of its teachers. So, of course, the sacraments must be rightly administered and the Word rightly preached and taught. People notice these things and pay attention to them. But if worship and instruction are not located in the body of Christ that is warmed by the love of Christ, most of us tend to look and listen elsewhere for some good news.

Speaking of looking and listening, the second factor that counts for spiritual growth and outreach is high quality instruction. Whether that Christian community is the congregation, the school where parents send their children, or the high school or college to which young people will commit years of energy and preparation for their future, the teacher and the teaching make the difference. Poll people about those who powerfully influenced their direction and beliefs in life, and they invariably include a teacher. So, too, for the church and its agencies. Following as a very close runner-up to the positive community factor, what draws and holds us to that community of believers is conspicuously good teaching of the faith.

This book examines the basics of what it takes to be that teacher and do that teaching. By "basics" we do not mean the technique of instructional delivery but, rather, the formation of what it takes to deliver a teacher of the church to the church. Teaching technique is well documented and anyone willing to do the homework and practice can acquire the "teacher effectiveness" skills to stand and deliver. The formation of a teacher of the church must certainly include that needed skill set, but it calls for much more than technique.

As we will see in chapter 2, to renew and restore Israel after the exile, Ezra "set his heart to study the law of the Lord, and to do it, and to teach the statutes and ordinances in Israel" (Ezra 7:10). Teaching the church is very much a matter of the heart—though not as the content of a Hallmark card. In Hebrew literature the heart is the locus of cognition, emotion, and judgment, that is, the coherent self. Thus, a teacher of the church is neither half-hearted nor double-minded.

The Apostle Paul insists that teaching the things of God means mastering a discipline and knowledge base: "And what you have heard me say in the presence of many witnesses entrust to reliable men who will also be qualified to teach others. . . . Do your best to present yourself to God as one approved, a workman who does not need to be ashamed and who correctly handles the word of truth" (2 Tim 2:2, 15). The teacher of the church has a body of knowledge to master which takes time and dedication, just as any discipline does.

Perhaps the most essential yet elusive trait for being a teacher of the church is self-resignation and endurance. Jesus cautions impulsive and reluctant followers in Matt 8:18–22 with his less-than-patient injunctions that "Foxes have holes and birds have nests, but the Son of man has no place to lay his head," and "Follow me, and leave the dead to bury their own dead." In Luke 9:62, he adds, "No one who puts his hand to the plow and looks back is fit for the kingdom of God." Sometimes, Jesus is just not very nice. Paul seems to have this attitude in mind when he urges that we deal with the world as though we have no dealings with it, for the form of this world is passing away (1 Cor 7:31; consider also Paul's interesting developmental sequence in Rom 5:1–5). As we will see in chapters 3 and 4, the teacher of the church certainly deals in the things of this world. But that teacher does so for the sake of a much bigger deal in the coming kingdom of God. Meanwhile, the teacher of the church does so without much interest in nicer holes and softer nests.

We have many teachers in the church, and they are a blessing for which we give thanks. Like Martha in Luke 10:38–42 and Tychicus in Col 4:7–9, they go about their tasks faithfully in loving service to others. Theirs is a genuine ministry of service in teaching an academic discipline, a subject area, a grade level, a Sunday school session, or a weekly Bible study. The aim of this book is the formation of more of those teachers *in* the church as teachers *of* the church. The teacher of the church conducts not only a ministry of service but also a ministry of that Word which is the whole counsel of God (Acts 20:27). To be or become such a teacher requires a clear sense of identity and a resolute sense of purpose. The chapters that follow can help with both of these characteristics.

Several people have assisted with providing that help. To keep the costs of the book to a minimum, the writers have made their work available free of charge and receive no royalties. Several of the chapters were previously published in *Lutheran Education Journal* and *Issues in Christian Education*. We thank the editors of those publications for permission to revise and reprint the essays. Thanks to those who read and critiqued some or all of the chapter drafts including Mark Blanke, Craig Parrott, Jerrald Pfabe, Martin Schmidt, Leah Schnare, Janell Uffelman, and Paul Vasconcellos. The authors also read and helped revise each other's work. Thanks to Jane Schaefer for electronically transcribing the previously published essays. Thanks to Kelly Russell for production assistance. And special thanks to Marlene Block for copy editing. Any errors at this point are now solely the responsibility of the editor.

We invite critique from readers. Comments may be sent to the editor at russ.moulds@cune.edu.

1

A Teacher of the Church

RUSS MOULDS

Dr. Moulds has served as a Lutheran high school teacher, college professor, and instructor in the parish. He writes and presents frequently on topics related to the teaching ministry. This chapter considers the question, "Who is a teacher of the church?"

WHATEVER YOUR image of "a teacher of the church" may be at this moment, expand that perception. In the chapters that follow, we will likely consider content related to your image, but to enlarge that view, consider first the history of the church and several examples of those who have served the teaching ministry, sometimes surprisingly so.

A Teacher Roster

In Acts 18, Priscilla and Aquila while at Ephesus encountered Apollos preaching about Jesus and detected he "knew only the baptism of John," so this wife-and-husband teaching team "took him and expounded to him the way of God more accurately." In third century AD Egypt, Antony, one of the church's first ascetic hermits or "desert fathers," attracted countless visitors and followers who frustrated his solitude by seeking to learn his simple Christian life. To the north in Syria, Symeon the Stylite concluded the church had become too worldly and needed an extreme lesson in discipleship, so he lived atop a pillar sixty feet closer to heaven.

In the tenth century, Peter Abelard—when he wasn't busy with his torrid, secret, and ultimately tragic love affair with his patron's daughter, Heloise—taught the church to re-read the earlier teachers of the church and reconsider its traditions, thus setting the stage for Luther and other reformers. When that time arrived, Philip Melanchthon, author of the

Augsburg Confession (and not a clergyman), extended his duties as a professor and activities as a reformer by opening a remedial school in his home for younger students who would not otherwise pass the university entrance exams.

In the twentieth century, Walter Becker (my first principal, whom you will not find in church history books) was called to move his teaching ministry to a new congregation where he and his wife and family resided on the stage in the school gymnasium for their first year until other housing could be arranged.

Not all these teachers are exemplars of ministry nor are any of their excesses a license for us. Yet their variety prompts us to ask: Who is a teacher of the church?

Who Is a Teacher of the Church?

In the context of these and other examples of the church's teachers, this book is aimed chiefly though not exclusively at those who are or soon will be teaching ministers in their congregations, schools, and colleges. The authors are all Lutherans with decades of service in the pastoral and teaching ministries. As a thinking reader, you will not agree with all the views presented here even as the authors do not all agree with each other. Nevertheless, this book will deepen your regard for the church's task of *didache*, the act of teaching Christians. The book explores what the writers believe are several key biblical texts and themes for teaching, selected doctrines of the church that inform teaching as a ministry, and features of teaching in the Lutheran tradition and its current practice. We authors address these matters with deep commitment to our shared Lutheran tradition, yet with profound respect for what the Holy Spirit has done across the centuries in other orthodox traditions of the Great Church.

If you don't happen to be of the Lutheran persuasion, we believe that examining this deep tradition with its strong emphasis on teaching the faith will enrich your understanding of your own tradition and your appreciation for our shared convictions within historical Christianity, that history acknowledged in this chapter's opening paragraphs. Welcome to our conversation, a conversation the church has shared—though not without dispute—for centuries.

A question not always explicitly asked in this conversation is, "Who is a teacher of the church?" That question may go unasked because its answer might be taken for granted. Some maintain that the theologians are the church's teachers. They must be included, yet most Christians do not hear or read the theologians and are influenced by them only indirectly as their ideas are filtered through local instruction, popular and simplified books, and sermons. Some say the pastors who preach those sermons are the church's teachers. Surely all pastoral acts serve to teach, but pastors are often the first to acknowledge that sermons (even in expository preaching) are not the best vehicle for instruction, that pastors are often not good instructors, and that their time is devoted to care for souls and church administration rather than teaching. The church has created such offices as director of Christian education or, in some congregations, minister of Christian nurture. Those in such offices sometimes teach, yet their responsibilities may revolve more around managing programs and facilitating activities which, though related to the church's *didache*, serve mostly as delivery systems for prepared materials and events.

Perhaps the teachers of the church today are the religious media figures, popular authors, and conference presenters. Without empirical studies, it's hard to say to what extent the church at large takes its cues from their content, though clearly some are influential. The quality of content varies with the source, and, while some of these high profile figures have much of value to offer, few are comprehensive in their scope. Most tend to focus on some specific concern, issue-oriented topic, or agenda for personal or congregational development, and, as always in the market place, the consumer's rule is *caveat emptor*. As a genuine teaching ministry, their greatest deficiency is the listener's lack of access to the dialog and mutual, interactive conversation that we see in the ministries of Jesus and Paul.

Another response to "Who is a teacher of the church?" limits the answer to Jesus and Paul and perhaps other biblical sources. By this account, Christ is the rabbi, his apostles are those sent to convey his teaching, we have their instruction in the New Testament which recognizes and includes the authority of the Old Testament (cf. Rom 15:4), and this is the source and norm for the church's teaching. Those who present their words are, then, not so much teachers as communicators. Certainly the historical church has assigned importance to this view with phrases such as *sola scriptura* and *solus Christus*. But ample biblical content also exists to validate some role, office, or function of teacher (see for example Eph 4:11–12 and 2 Tim 2:2), as we will confirm in later chapters.

Given that biblical content, some role for the teacher has existed in the church from its earliest years. Thus, another answer to who our teachers are could be called the patristic view. The "patristics," or "church fathers," refer to those church thinkers and writers in the first several Christian centuries who hammered out the doctrinal positions that define our historical orthodoxy. The shape of our teaching today was put in place by teachers such as Origen, Athanasius, and Augustine as they thought deeply, originally, creatively, and sometimes controversially in order to separate truth from error in what the Christian faith says and means. Their individual efforts were not always successful, and they found plenty of fault with each other along the way, but cumulatively their work yielded a body of instruction that the church has since relied on and continues to affirm.[1]

But not indiscriminantly. The Roman Catholic church and the Protestant churches divided 500 years ago in part over how much authority to assign to the church fathers and their traditions. This is a dispute that every teacher of the church today—Lutheran, Catholic, or otherwise—should learn, appreciate, and be ready to discuss with students because it involves the authority of the Gospel itself. The reader will have to pursue that complex story in other studies, but here it points to an additional view: since church teachers do not always agree, the real teacher of the church is the Holy Spirit. Only the Holy Spirit, the Paraclete (John 14:16), can give us insight to the Scriptures, help us glean truths from the church fathers, the church's traditions, and other church figures past and present, and guide us to what God would have us know. But this view, in turn, raises age-old problems about excessive subjectivism and individualism for the Christian learner. The Christian, whether learner or teacher, is also a member of the body of Christ and the whole faith community in which God is at work. We not only say, "*I* believe in God the Father almighty," but also "*Our* Father who art in heaven."[2]

Teaching the Community of Christ

Teaching the church, then, is a community role, and that role includes those teaching in the Christian community's congregations, schools, and colleges. Yet in my own work in Lutheran high schools, colleges, and church worker conferences, I find that many who are such teachers do not consider themselves a "teacher of the church." Rather, by their perception, they are certainly faithful Christians and teach the fourth grade in a parish school but are not teachers of their congregation; or they teach a subject and coach a sport in a church-affiliated high school but not the things of

1. We continue to hear about some of the theological fringe elements that the church fathers addressed and refuted (Gnosticism is an example) as today's popular culture rediscovers some of their writings in library archives and an occasional old manuscript is found and published.

2. The original Greek in the Nicene Creed begins, "*We* believe in God the Father almighty."

faith; or they profess their discipline in a college with a denominational connection but don't teach or explicitly locate their teaching within that theological tradition; or they run educational programs for their congregation, but they are program administrators and not expositors of Scripture as a means of grace; or they are competent shepherds and preachers but, though they are supposed to be apt teachers (2 Tim 3:2), haven't the time or training to develop curriculum that fosters disciples.

"Teacher of the church"—the expression sounds a bit grandiose. Who would be so bold as to claim it? Instead, we should join Paul in his self-identity as chief of sinners. True enough. Whoever would teach the Christian faith and life must do so with the self-effacing humility of sinner-saint rather than any pride of office.

What's more, perhaps our congregational and educational practitioners' belief is correct. Perhaps they are not teachers of the church if they don't have, in addition to a practical grasp of the Gospel, a good command of a) Scripture, b) the church's history, c) its hermeneutic tools, d) its doctrines, e) their own and different traditions, f) current spiritual issues and influences in their community, and g) some effective ways of educing spiritual growth in that community. Now, that may sound like a tall order, but think about some lesser degree of expertise next time you're sitting in a dentist's chair or airliner.

And what if we don't have teachers who are competent in these characteristics? Just as nature hates a vacuum, the same is true of the spiritual reality. The priests of Baal (1 Kgs 18), Simon Magus (Acts 8), and the "super apostles" (2 Cor 11) are always ready to step in and fill a teaching void. Teaching of some sort will always occur in or be directed at the church. The question is: Who will the teachers be and what will they teach?

The church, then, will have to identify its teachers. And the church has prepared candidates among those already in its congregations, schools, and colleges. Many may not consider themselves teachers of the church. But many of them could be, and already are or are prepared to become such teachers. That's what this book is about. We offer perspective, background, comment, reflection, and some positions we stake out along the way. We hope to encourage those who serve in some practice of teaching *in the church* to serve also as teachers *of the church*. As the Holy Spirit calls, gathers, enlightens, and sanctifies the whole Christian church, by that church God also calls out those he will use to instruct the church so that we may "grow in the grace and knowledge of our Lord and Savior Jesus Christ" (2 Pet 3:18). We will examine this calling—both the role and the process—thoroughly in later chapters.

At this point in this chapter, the reader might expect some dramatic alarm about some crisis for the church or the teaching ministry, and why we'd better do something soon about this dire condition. However, alarm is not in order: "Built on the Rock, the church will stand, even while steeples are falling." Yet neither is complacency: "Hark, the voice of Jesus calling." And when calling the apostles, he assures them, "On this rock I will build my church, and the gates of hell shall not prevail against it" (Matt 16:18).

No Small Potatoes

Think of it this way: for two thousand years, the church has withstood the persecution of the Roman Empire, numerous heresies, several attempts at intellectual takeovers such as modernism, progressivism, and fascism, the moral erosion of consumerism, the threat of world communism, and its own share of internal scandals and corruption. The church is not going away, and those teaching in the church are not part of a small-potatoes operation, even though your congregation or school or college may seem like it. The point is, we not only have the Gospel to teach, we also have much to teach about the Gospel. The faith we teach is two thousand years old, global and transcultural, and greater than any government, science, commerce, or intellectual movement that has or will come along. This book is not, then, a wake-up call, a serving of notice, or a shrill screed of warning. It's a gentle reminder and invitation to hear the church's need and call for teachers of God's Word and respond to that call especially in one's own locale.

Teaching the Church in the World:
Five Current Conditions

Still, while the Gospel remains the same (Heb 13:8), every age in the church has its challenges, dangers, and opportunities, and so its conditions for ministry change as well. Five cultural themes will likely influence the conditions for the teaching ministry in the decades to come. Those conditions will impact who the church recognizes and calls as its teachers and how our teaching is carried out. The themes are as complex as culture itself and are the subject of much attention (and might be numbered differently or more than five). We briefly note these to acknowledge both the church and the world as our context for teaching and to keep in mind in later chapters, bearing also in mind that predictions are not prophecy.

1. De-concentration of public education's near-monopoly is altering how people perceive school, teaching, teachers, learning, and education. By and large, "teaching" for most people is still synonymous with public school teaching as it has been for about a hundred years, but that baseline is now shifting. Parochial and Christian schools continue to grow in number. Jewish and Muslim schools, though not numerous, are a bigger part of the mix. Home schooling continues to increase. Public schools experiment with hybrids such as charter schools and commercially managed school districts. For now, teaching ministers in parochial schools (and teaching ministry students) inaccurately continue to compare their activities with public school teachers rather than their fellow ministers of the Gospel. However, what has been the traditional neighborhood public school will no longer be the standard by which we begin our thinking about teaching and education. That predisposition will change as the educational landscape changes, and with it comes the opportunity to rethink what we mean and expect about the teacher of the church.[3]

2. A culture always presumes some world view. In our society, that monopoly no longer belongs to the church as it once did. Competition is increasing for who gets to tell the grand narrative of life. Contestants include institutionalized science, the popular media, and political movements as well as the church. Versions of the human story include various forms of post-modernism, evolution, materialistic naturalism, genetic human enhancement, political-religious fundamentalism, and world environmental and economic collapse or perhaps culminating balance. The teacher of the church pays attention to the current idolatries that would substitute some lesser vision of the human story for what God is doing in the world through Christ. The teacher of the church has a comprehensive narrative that claims to contain all the other stories in Jesus: "For God has put all things in subjection under him" (1 Cor 15:27).

3. Radical Islam is provoking a cautious and even negative perception of conservative religion in general. While some will interpret the activities and clashes of fundamentalist movements in terms of authentic spiritual warfare, others will lump together all religion and especially conservative religion as a source of conflict rather than hope. The teacher of the church

---

3. Even a little reading in the history and policy of education, public and private, in the United States reveals its Byzantine complexities. Higher education is part of this history and current change. We are seeing smaller colleges attrition in the competition, research universities build alliances with corporations, the Internet and other venues take some instructional roles though not as expected, and costs continue to rise faster than the economy's inflation rate.

will have the task of interpreting these developments in Scripture's terms of sin, judgment, and grace and representing historical, orthodox Christianity as hopeful and life-affirming rather than hostile and destructive.

4. The Southern Cross—a night sky's constellation we Northerners never see—is rising as the worldwide center of gravity for Christianity now rapidly moves to the Southern Hemisphere. The Christendom of Europe is gone. American Christianity is stable for the time being but not growing. Africa, South America, and Southeast Asia will be home to what Philip Jenkins calls "the next Christianity."[4] He anticipates and is troubled that "the twenty-first century will be regarded by future historians as a century in which religion replaces ideology as the prime animating and destructive force in human affairs." The concern is that the new emerging churches will neglect the continued reformation of the church (the Latin phrase is *ecclesia semper reformanda*, the church is always reforming) over the past 500 years and will needlessly and tragically rerun much of the worst of the older church's history. We do not want to repeat the denominational warfare of earlier centuries. While teaching ministers chiefly attend to their own local efforts, at least some teachers of the church will need to consider their ministry at a larger and even global scale for those new churches who could learn from our collective experience.

5. Closer to home, our own society and economy is undergoing increased polarization of the wealthy and the lower income stratum. Church workers who serve at the lower income level that comes with the office will find themselves distanced from the comparatively comfortable circumstances of their parents and grandparents. Many already seem to be struggling with financial responsibility, retirement planning, debt, attitudes and expectations about standard of living in a consumer economy, and what the teacher's own financial conduct teaches the church. Luther reminds us, "Good works do not make a Christian, but a Christian makes good works." The teacher's responsible (though not legalistic) stewardship of personal finances, especially in a consumer economy, is a good and responsible work. Surely, others learn as much from what a teacher of the church does—in this case regarding mammon—as what that teacher says. In our culture, this may become a hard lesson for teaching ministers to learn and then teach.[5]

---

4. Jenkins, *The Next Christendom*. See also his summary of this thesis, "The Next Christianity," in *The Atlantic Monthly*, October 2002.

5. For discussion on personal debt among church workers, see *Issues in Christian Education*, "Church Worker Indebtedness: a Search for Solutions," Vol. 40, No. 3, Winter 2006.

An Enlarged Image

The following chapters do not explore these sorts of societal themes, but such matters are never far from this book's topics. We encourage the reader to keep these and similar themes in mind for an enlarged understanding of today's teaching ministry. The chapters will put in place a collection of basic biblical concepts and practices for the teacher of the church discussed not by one but seven authors who have been blessed to be part of that ministry.

The usual problem with a collection of essays from several writers is the lack of a uniform style and voice. In this case, we think the variety is an asset that reflects "the varieties of gifts, but the same Spirit, the varieties of service, but the same Lord, and the varieties of working, but the same God who works them all in everyone . . . for the common good" (1 Cor 12:4–7). We hope you will appreciate the different ways that different contributors can express different views on the same authentic ministry of teaching. There are some common and essential elements in the church's task of *didache*, the act of teaching Christians, but there is no one monolithic model for being a teacher of the church. Therefore, the next chapter—our exegetical study—presents a survey of several teaching texts from Scripture yet with consistent encouragement to teach the Scriptures and Christ who is their center. The Bible is the right place to commence a study of the teaching ministry.

2

Christian Teaching:
That They May Have Life Abundantly

CHARLES BLANCO

Professor Blanco has served as a parish pastor, director of pre-seminary
studies, and professor of Greek and Biblical interpretation. He is highly
regarded for bringing Word and life together in his preaching and teaching.
This chapter provides an exegetical context for the teaching ministry.

"For Ezra had set his heart to study the law of the LORD, and
to do it, and to teach the statutes and ordinances in Israel."
(Ezra 7:10)[1]

To DESCRIBE the former teacher as "inadequate" would be charitable.
Closer to the truth was "incompetent." After half a year the students
had made no progress whatsoever. In fact, for many of them, regress was
the appropriate term. It was not just instructional content that was lack-
ing. The atmosphere was toxic. Mutual care and respect among students
was absent. Good students had taken up bad practices and poor students
had conformed themselves to even lower standards. Enthusiasm for learning was nil.

And now *you* are the mid-year teaching replacement. Where in the
world do you start? The situation is twisted from every vantage point. You
suppose that you could just call it hopeless. It wouldn't be your fault. No
one would hold you responsible for what has happened. You could just
coast through the end of the year and pass these students on to someone

---

1. The present passage comes from the *New Revised Standard Version*. Unless otherwise
indicated, Scripture references in the remainder of the chapter are to the *New International
Version*.

else to worry about. Besides, this class is going to hate you for the changes you will have to make to salvage the rest of the year. Why not save yourself and them a lot of grief and just maintain the *status quo?* You'll get paid the same no matter what, right?

Career? Calling!

But that's not your *calling*, is it? You're not just a contracted employee. You have a *Christian vocation.* Not simply from the Board of Education (although they were involved), but more importantly, from *God!* From your Creator and your Redeemer. From the Lord who counted you so valuable to himself that in spite of your sins and shortcomings, he died to give you life. This same Lord counts every student in your new class just as valuable as you. Your Savior has brought you to this time and place. Coast? Just put in your time? It's tempting, but ultimately unthinkable. You are a *Christian* teacher. You have a calling. Thus, under the shadow of the cross and in the light of the resurrection and by the power of the Spirit who makes dry bones come to life, you set yourself to work.

Change a few details in this scenario and your name is Ezra. You are a priest of Israel living in exile in Babylonia. Some of your people have returned to the homeland of Judah. Yet, over the course of time they have grown lax in their faith and life. Their actions are threatening the continuance of the covenant promise made to Abraham. There is a great need for reform. But the reforms called for won't be popular (imagine carrying out the actions described in Ezra 9–10, the intentional divorcing of spouses from one another for spiritual reasons—hardly the stuff that wins popularity contests!). Yet, Ezra's vocation was just that, to leave his familiar routine in Babylonia and go through much anguish of body and soul for the sake of his God and God's people. Where would he start?

Check the italicized verse at the beginning of the chapter.[2] Note the four elements involved in Ezra's approach, elements appropriate for every Christian teacher to employ:

1. *Ezra set his heart.* There are many technical skills teachers must learn to be effective. These are good and useful and ought not be despised. But what sets a Christian teacher apart (whether in a parochial or secular setting) is preparation of the heart. In the Bible the heart is not only the seat of emotions and feelings, but also the seat of the will and intellect

---

2. I am indebted to Dr. Katheryn L. Webb of Trinity Theological Seminary in Newburgh, Indiana, for indicating the significance of this verse for the teaching task.

and belief.[3] Ezra comprehended with Jeremiah (17:9) and Jesus (Matt 15:17–20) that, as God addresses us through the Law, the heart is the primary problem within us and must be the first thing we address (daily) in carrying out our calling (Matt 5:8). The teacher called by God through the Gospel draws near to the Lord with the heart, confessing humbly that it is the Spirit of God who draws us to himself and renews us for service (Gal 4:4–7).

2. *To study the Law of the Lord.* There is a specific and revealed content that guides and directs a Christian teacher's attitudes and actions. It is to that content that we return for refreshment and encouragement, correction and direction regularly. The Hebrew word for "Law" in this passage is *torah*, which might be better translated as "instruction," "revelation," "teaching." That is, while Lutheran ears are trained to understand "law" in its accusatory, sin-revealing sense (and it surely always does that), *torah* in its biblical usage can also encompass "Gospel," the good news of God's grace toward us.[4] Thus, what Ezra determined to do is not simply study God's "rule book," but more fully he determined to inform his heart with the fullness of God's wisdom regarding how to proceed, which would include acts of both Law and Gospel.

3. *To do it.* Is there anything more hollow than an instructor who ignores his own instruction? Ezra comprehended that simply to study and to know is insufficient in light of his *calling.* He was called also to act, to do, to practice what he would teach. In what follows in this essay we shall see how intimately connected are *knowing* and *doing* in the biblical understanding of what is involved in teaching and learning. For technical reasons of study we distinguish the *cognitive* from *praxis* (the practice of skills),

---

3. For a sampling of passages showing that the heart deals with more than feelings, see Ps 33:11; 51:10; 90:12; Prov 4:20–23; 16:9; 18:15; Luke 2:19; 6:45; Rom 6:17–18; 10:6–10.

4. See, for example, Ps 19:7 where the law (*torah*) of the Lord *revives* the soul (and is, hence, *Gospel* activity). Or see Ps 78:1, where *torah* is translated as "teaching," which, in the context of the psalm, has to do with God's *gracious* dealings with his stiff-necked people. In Jer 31:33, a section dealing with the *new* covenant, it is the *torah* that God puts in believers' hearts, which in full biblical understanding we interpret as "Gospel." This is not to say *torah* always has this sense, but when, for instance, the psalmist declares that he loves the Law of the Lord (119:97), he is not simply saying that he loves to be chastised with the revelation of his sins (although in light of the Gospel we see that such an event is necessary and "good"); rather, the psalmist is proclaiming a love for all that God has revealed in his Word—both Law and Gospel—without which we would be in the dark concerning his mercy and grace and wisdom. For a helpful summary, see the entry for *torah* in *Theological Wordbook of the Old Testament*, 2 vols., edited by R. Laird Harris, Gleason L. Archer, Jr., and Bruce K. Waltke (Chicago: Moody Press, 1980) 1:403–5.

but biblically speaking, it is a distinction that must never become a sharp separation in daily life (sometimes called "dead orthodoxy" in Christian circles).

4. *To teach the statutes and ordinances in Israel.* The issue at hand was not what would make Ezra's life or the life of the Israelites pleasant and conflict-free. Wouldn't we all wish all our days to be like that? However, in a sin-corrupted world, in a world where God has called his people to be his light shining in the *darkness* (Matt 5:14–16; Phil 2:15), the issue is that we teach what God calls us to teach, even when such content will not always or immediately be welcomed. Further, Ezra's vocation was to do that teaching *in Israel*, not in the comfort of his residence in Babylonia. In Christian ministry we don't get to choose who will be members of our parishes or our classrooms. It would have been much easier for Ezra to hand select a group of sanctified Israelites and teach them. However, God calls us to work with those of his choosing, not ours. Our Savior's purpose was to "seek and to save *the lost*" (Luke 19:10; Matt 9:12). Can we seek other?

Thus, when we think of our Christian calling (in this case, the vocation of Christian teacher), we understand that the response to this calling involves a heart captive to the Lord's instruction (*torah*, both Law and Gospel), a life that strives to live in harmony with that instruction,[5] and a determination to convey his Word of life for the temporal and eternal benefit of others. Although this task is daunting and leaves us wondering about our adequacy for it, the Christian teacher has gifts from God at his or her disposal that are wholly sufficient for the carrying out of this ministry (Eph 3:20–21; 4:7–16). Therefore, as we take up our task, we join with the Apostle in declaring, "Not that we are competent of ourselves to claim anything as coming from us; our competence is from God" (2 Cor 3:5). In the confidence that God provides in Christ, we, like Ezra before us, proceed where we would otherwise fear to tread.

---

5. Always a work in progress due to the on-going struggle of saint and sinner within (Rom 7:15—8:2)—thank God our justification does not depend on *our* success in this struggle!

Teaching in the Scriptures

To "get a handle" on the task of the Christian teacher, we turn ourselves to an analysis of the use of the term "teach" (including its cognates) in the Bible.[6]

Teaching: A Divine Activity

The first and most important observation we may make is that God is never on the "learner" end of the teacher-learner spectrum. In Scripture, whenever the term is used in connection with God, he is always the teacher. How could it be other? God is omniscient! Thus, whenever the topic is even addressed in the Bible, it is done so by means of rhetorical question, as in Isaiah 40:14, "Whom did the LORD consult to enlighten him, and who taught him the right way? Who was it that taught him knowledge or showed him the path of understanding?"[7] It is a characteristic of God, then, that he teaches.

Not surprisingly, in the New Testament Jesus is presented as *the* Teacher (often addressed that way, for example in Luke 10:25; also he is "Rabbi" to his disciples, for example John 4:31). In summing up Jesus' activity on earth, teaching is one of the primary descriptors of his ministry.[8] Nearly one quarter of the occurrences of "teach" and its cognates in the Bible have to do with Jesus as the teacher. A simple answer to, "What Would Jesus Do?" is "Teach!"

As we shall see, not all human teaching is divine teaching, but it is humbling and inspiring to consider that to engage in the task of teaching is to engage in something that God himself does. When you stand at the head of your classroom, don't forget to tingle.

---

6. Other words used of the teaching task in the Bible are typically translated as: instruct, guide, lead, direct, train, equip, explain. An examination of each of these words would be profitable, but is beyond the scope of this article. The author commends to the reader a concordance study on each of these terms. The logic is compelling that a person heeding the call of the Christian teaching ministry would have spent time looking at every passage in the Bible that describes teaching. There are slightly over 400 verses in which "teach" or a cognate occurs. That's a lot, but not insurmountable. What are you waiting for?

7. See also Job 21:22 and Rom 11:33–36. Some significant passages in which God is the teacher include: Exod 4:12–15; Ps 25:4–9; 32:8; 119:12 (and 11 other times in this pedagogically significant psalm); Isa 48:17; Hos 11:1–3.

8. As a mere sampling, see Matt 4:23; 9:35; Mark 4:2; John 18:20; Acts 1:1.

Teaching: A Democratic Activity

A second observation is how many different grammatical subjects are used for "teach" and its cognates. Most of these grammatical subjects are persons, but some are impersonal.[9] Excluding references to the Trinity, one may count some 50 different persons/groups cited as performing the teaching task in Scripture. They include:

- the famous (for example, Moses, David, John the Baptist, Saul/Paul)
- the infamous (for example, Pharisees, Sadducees, Scribes/teachers of the law, Judaizers)
- the holy (for example, Aaron, priests, Levites)
- the unholy (for example, idols, images, false teachers, Philistines, pagan nations, demons)
- the obscure (for example, Bezalel and Oholiab,[10] Manaen[11])
- the familial (for example, mother, father, parents)
- the ecclesiastical (for example, disciples, apostles, overseers, elders, Timothy, Titus)[12]

9. Among the impersonal "teachers" are animals (Job 12:7), earth (Job 12:8), nature (1 Cor 11:14), the act of church discipline (1 Tim 1:20).

10. Chief engineers for the construction of the tabernacle in the wilderness (Exod 35:30–35).

11. One of the teachers in the church in Antioch (Acts 13:1), of whom we know nothing else in the Bible except that he was raised in the household of Herod the tetrarch.

12. One feels compelled to address briefly the issue of women teaching in the church. Women are found to be teachers in a number of passages: Prov 3:1; 6:20; 31:1; Song 8:2; Jer 9:20; Titus 2:3–4. There are also specific restrictions about the scope within which a woman is permitted to teach (1 Tim 2:9–15; 1 Cor 14:33–35). Those texts notwithstanding, the Scriptures do speak of certain women engaged in teaching the Christian faith, most pointedly Priscilla (Acts 18:26, where the verb is usually translated "explained"; the same verb is used of St. Paul's address in Acts 28:23, where teaching of the Christian faith is clearly taking place).

While there is some ambiguity and lack of specific detail in the following passages, it is clear that Paul held a significant number of women in the highest regard with respect to their service in the church, and the language he uses hardly suggests he was thinking in terms of preparing food for the congregational pot-luck supper. We may cite: Phoebe (Rom 16:1), Mary (Rom 16:6), Tryphena and Tryphosa (Rom 16:12), Persis (Rom 16:12), Euodia and Syntyche (Phil 4:2–3, where Paul comments that both these women "contended at my side for the cause of the Gospel," suggesting a substantial amount of sacrifice and toil and, in light of Paul's history, risk of personal harm).

I believe my own church body, The Lutheran Church—Missouri Synod (LCMS) has made an honest effort to deal honorably with all that the Scriptures say about women teaching in the church, and have thereby understood the restrictions mentioned above as being *not* general in nature (prohibiting any kind of teaching), but as having specific reference to the office of the public ministry, the pastoral office. Where there is no subversion of

All this is to say that the activity of teaching is not caste-like. This is important for those who are about to enter a "caste" ("commissioned minister") to remember. While you are receiving special training in Christian doctrine and practice and in the formal skills of teaching, your students will be taught by many, many individuals. Don't imagine that you and you alone are qualified to teach. A teacher who approaches a parent as if the parent is perhaps a necessary but unfortunate addition to the child's educational life will not only be offensive, but is denying an essential biblical truth concerning the role of parents.[13]

Therefore, wherever it is possible, see your place as working alongside others for the well-being of your students. However, the Christian teacher, in light of specialized training received, is in a position to provide unique blessings to students.

Teaching: A Powerful Activity

When one considers the various metaphors associated with "teach" and its cognates, one is struck by how potent the Scriptures regard the teaching task to be. Teaching is compared to the rain and dew that water the earth (Deut 32:2), a fountain of life (Prov 13:14), a lamp and light in darkness (Prov 6:23), yeast that leavens a large amount of flour (Matt 16:12), wind

the pastoral office, the Scriptures do not prohibit a woman from teaching the faith.

Some specific issues in this area are still being explored in the LCMS. There would appear now to be a general agreement in the Synod that no issue exists regarding a woman teaching religion in a Christian elementary school. However, questions exist with regard to other settings. "May a woman teach confirmation?" Many congregations engage in this practice (and it may increase with growing numbers of women serving as DCEs); however, some strongly hold that teaching confirmation is the task of the pastor alone. "May a woman be called to teach theology at the high school level?" Currently, yes, but there are Lutheran high schools where local school boards/associations allow only men to teach theology/religion courses. "May a woman be called to teach theology at the collegiate or seminary level?" Currently, no. "May a woman be called to teach history or 'practical/methods' courses at the collegiate or seminary level in which theology is a significant component of the instructional content?" This is happening in the LCMS, but not, apparently, within any Theology Department *per se*.

For further reading, see the following documents produced by the LCMS Commission on Theology and Church Relations (CTCR), available from Concordia Publishing House (St. Louis, MO) and from the LCMS web site (www.lcms.org): *Woman Suffrage and the Church* (1968); *Women in the Church* (1985); *The Service of Women in Congregational and Synodical Offices* (1994). As this present volume is being published, it is my understanding that another CTCR document on the roles of men and women in the church is in preparation.

13. See, for example, Deut 4:9–10; Prov 1:8; 3:1; 4:2. We further recognize that parents can also be one of the sources of sin in the lives of students and teachers.

that can drive a ship (Eph 4:14). False teaching is compared to gangrene (2 Tim 2:17).[14]

A teacher and a body of teaching are recognized as having the potential to impact a life in the utmost of ways. While this is true in the generic sense of teaching, it is all the more true with Christian teaching, where one is dealing with the very Word of life.

It is perhaps because the teaching task is recognized as very powerful in its impact upon others that there are warnings in the Scriptures about aspiring to this ministry. Focusing specifically upon the teaching of Christian doctrine (surely in the purview of a Lutheran school teacher or DCE), James warns, "Not many of you should presume to be teachers, my brothers, because you know that we who teach will be judged more strictly" (James 3:1). Jesus reserves some of his harshest criticism for those who wanted to be honored as teachers in the community (Matt 23:1–33; more succinctly, Luke 20:46–47; less caustically but just as crushing, John 3:1–12).

Aside from the sheer responsibility associated with the task of Christian teaching, one also recognizes the fact that when a teacher and a student "connect" so that learning takes place, it is greatly gratifying to the teacher's ego. There is a "rush" that could easily become an addiction, so much so that a teacher might confuse this ancillary outcome with the primary outcome, and thus alter one's focus from serving God and student to serving self. The verses cited in the previous paragraph are intended to warn us from that end by having us see how susceptible we are to the abuse of the position and its power. Of course, these verses should not be read to the exclusion of God's promises to work through "jars of clay" (2 Cor 4:7). We recall that God overcame Moses' self-doubt and inadequacies (Exod 4:10–17). Nevertheless, one should not enter the Christian teaching ministry without serious reflection.

Heed the warning, all teachers in training: handle with care. An explosive device in the hands of an expert can clear away debris so that what is built up is good and useful. An explosive device in the hands of an incompetent (even worse, one with selfish, evil intent), however, can do grave harm. A "truth virus" released in students can enter every fiber of their being for a lifetime of blessing, but the virus of error, once it has infected our thought processes, can be extremely difficult to eradicate.

14. Consider the implication of such a description in the pre-antibiotic age of the New Testament. Even today, gangrene is feared and is not always controllable, leading to amputation of limbs. Imagine the fear occasioned by its onset two millennia ago. Such is the fear of allowing false teaching to go unchecked in the church.

Although no one will be a "perfect" teacher, God directs us to be careful so that what we teach is true, right, good, edifying, and above all, God-pleasing.

Teaching: God's or Man's?

Not far beneath the surface of nearly all the Bible's information on teaching is the question of this sub-section. God created humans with the capacity to learn, and he blessed that activity in the Garden (Gen 1:28). However, as the events of the fall into sin illustrate, humans are also able to be misled, to be taught wrongly.[15] The story of the fall into sin is that we humans prefer our own ideas to God's, even when that preference results in death (Rom 1:21ff).[16]

In one sense, the act of teaching is neutral, neither good nor evil in itself. The question has to do with the *content* of what is taught. Instructional methods courses are certainly important, as is classroom training and experience. However, from the perspective of Christian vocation, what is essential is teaching that which is in harmony with God's revealed will made known chiefly through the Word (2 Tim 3:14–17), and specifically through the Word made flesh (Jesus; John 1:1–18), brought to us by the ministry of Christ's Spirit (John 14:6; 15:26; 16:12–15).

Any number of passages can be cited that urge the teaching of God's truth and warn against substituting for it what appears wise to humans but is in fact contrary to God's will. The situation was acute in both Old[17] and New[18] Testaments.

---

15. We note that this is true even when the teacher is excellent: God taught Adam and Eve, and still they turned from him. Similarly, Jesus taught the Twelve, and still they deserted him. There is some (little) solace for teachers (and parents) in this fact, that even though our teaching may be engaging, stimulating, and accurate, still, there is no guarantee of the learning outcome. Prov 22:6 ("Train a child in the way he should go and when he is old he will not depart from it") is just that, a proverb, a general truth, not a binding contract assuring a specific result.

16. All Scripture is true, but after several decades of church work I would profess there is no truer Scriptural passage than Isaiah 55:8–9: "'For my thoughts are not your thoughts, neither are your ways my ways,' declares the LORD. 'As the heavens are higher than the earth, so are my ways higher than your ways and my thoughts than your thoughts.'"

17. Examples include: Deut 4:1; 4:14; 5:31; 6:1; 1 Kings 8:36; Ps 86:11; Isa 2:3. For examples of avoiding false teachings, see Deut 20:17–18; Mal 2:7–9.

18. Examples include: Matt 28:20; John 8:31–32; Titus 2:12. For examples of avoiding false teachings, see Matt 5:19; 2 Thess 3:6; Rev 2:20. For a longer assessment of the issue of human wisdom vs. the wisdom of God in Christ Jesus, see 1 Cor 1:18—2:16.

A passage that concentrates our focus because it is found in the Old Testament and quoted by Jesus in the New is Isa 29:13, "The Lord says: 'These people come near to me with their mouth and honor me with their lips, but their hearts are far from me. Their worship of me is made up only of rules taught by men'" (see its use by Jesus in Matt 15:2–9 and Mark 7:2–13). Knowledge and wisdom developed by human investigation are not inherently wicked, but human teaching that obscures or replaces divine teaching is at heart demonic. Jesus' point is that we humans are prone to abuse any teaching for our own purposes, advantage, and glory. It need not be an evil teaching (the idea of gifts dedicated to God in the Matt 15 passage has a good origin of godly devotion[19]); sinful humans can corrupt anything (2 Pet 3:16–17).

Therefore, the Christian teacher has the special responsibility before God of weighing the content of what is being taught to see if it shrouds the light of God's truth (1 John 4:1). If it does, the error must be exposed, no matter how popular or attractive or winning the subject matter is. This applies to Christian doctrine most fully (Titus 2:1). We take note that Paul did not mind repeating this warning to Timothy frequently in his correspondence with him.[20]

However, it is also the case that we may mislead people by the manner of our life and conduct. The chief concern of a Christian teacher is, "Can people see Christ and his Gospel foremost in my life and ministry?" The charge the high priest leveled against the Apostles in Acts was this, "We gave you strict orders not to teach in this name [the name of Jesus] . . . Yet you have filled Jerusalem with your teaching" (Acts 5:28). In spite of the Sanhedrin's charge to cease and desist, "Day after day, in the temple courts and from house to house, they [the Apostles] never stopped teaching and proclaiming the good news that Jesus is the Christ" (Acts 5:42). The biblically consistent principle Peter set before the high priest was this: "We must obey God rather than men" (Acts 5:29).

This is the ultimate concern of those who are Christian teachers, that in everything they say and do, day by day, they bear witness that Jesus is the Christ. C. F. W. Walther reminds us, the Gospel must predominate.[21]

---

19. See the material in Lev 27 on things dedicated and devoted to the Lord.

20. See 1 Tim 1:3; 1:7; 4:2; 6:3; 2 Tim 2:17; 4:3. While one of the characteristics of ministry within the LCMS is a concern for sound teaching and pure doctrine, we also want to heed Paul's warnings about getting into disputes that are really only wars about words (1 Tim 1:3–7; 2 Tim 2:23; Titus 3:8–11).

21. See his 25th thesis in *The Proper Distinction between Law and Gospel*, trans. W. H. T. Dau (St. Louis: Concordia, 1928).

When people observe your teaching situation, will they conclude in short order that Jesus is the Head of the class? Will they conclude that Christ is the center of your teaching? Will they conclude that this is the place where the Gospel predominates? If not, we honor him only with our lips, while our hearts are far from him, as we have allowed the teachings of men to replace the teachings of Christ. Then it is time for a repentant return to the cross, wherein Jesus makes all things new (2 Cor 5:17).

Teaching: The Goal Is Action

Our final observation about the use of "teach" in the Scriptures has to do with how often it is connected to "doing," to activity. To be sure, there is a place in the Scriptures for cerebral activity (Ps 77:12: "I will meditate on all your works"), but what the data amply illustrate is that biblical teaching is to eventuate in action, in service of God and neighbor.[22]

Paradigmatic from the Old Testament is Deut 6:1, Moses' parting words to the Israelites: "These are the commands, decrees and laws the LORD your God directed me to teach you to observe in the land that you are crossing the Jordan to possess." To achieve a cognitive goal only would have been insufficient. The point is to teach the Israelites to *observe* God's decrees. It must be noted, certainly, that Israel's actual observance of these decrees was woeful (a conclusion I reach about my own performance daily). However, the point still stands: biblical "religion" is not only a matter of interiority; it is also about exterior living for his glory.[23]

Paradigmatic from the New Testament is Matt 28:19–20, the Great Commission, which reads in part, "teaching them to obey everything I have commanded you." Christian teaching has as a goal obedience to the teachings of Christ. Grace and faith surely are prerequisite for salvation (Eph 2:8–9), but works are the product of genuine faith (Eph 2:10). Fully congruent with the Old Testament understanding, Jesus included in his teaching this mandate: "A new command I give you: Love one another. As I have loved you, so you must love one another. By this all men will know that you are my disciples, if you love one another" (John 13:34–35).[24]

22. Among passages linking teaching with observing, following, obeying, etc. are Deut 4:1; 5:31; Ps 86:11; 90:12; 119:33; 143:10; John 8:31–32; John 15:20; Titus 2:12. There are also passages that warn against false teaching precisely because such teaching leads to sinful activity: Deut 20:18; Rev 2:20.

23. Thus, James 1:27: "Religion that God our Father accepts as pure and faultless is this: to look after orphans and widows in their distress and to keep oneself from being polluted by the world."

24. Echoed by St. Paul in Rom 13:8–10.

We are reminded that the way to bring about this new living is by teaching continually about the source of our new life, Jesus Christ, crucified and raised from the dead. It is the Gospel that enables the keeping of the Law: "We love him because he first loved us" (1 John 4:19). The biblical pattern in Old and New Testaments is that the *indicative* (the statement that God loves us) precedes and supports the *imperative* (the command that we are to follow).[25]

It is in this regard that we note Paul's words to Titus, "In everything set them an example by doing what is good. In your teaching show integrity, seriousness, and soundness of speech that cannot be condemned, so that those who oppose you may be ashamed because they have nothing bad to say about us" (Titus 2:7–8). In Paul's view, teaching good content is certainly required, but so is teaching by good example. The Christian teacher will have as his or her goal, then, not only speaking the truth of Christ, but living the truth of Christ as well. This will be evident, for example, in:

- the manner in which students, colleagues, administrators, parents, etc. are treated
- the manner and the goal for which discipline is rendered
- the manner in which conflicts are handled
- how the teacher is seen behaving outside of the classroom
- how the teacher speaks about money, glory, success, etc.

Will such actions be in accord with God's teachings or human (i.e., corrupted) longings? It is the Christian teacher's desire that students will be impacted by both *what* is taught and *how* the teaching takes place. In this fashion, the Christian teacher's goals are congruent with the Savior's: "I came that they may have life, and have it abundantly" (John 10:10).

Conclusion

"When Jesus landed and saw a large crowd, he had compassion on them, because they were like sheep without a shepherd. So he began teaching them many things" (Mark 6:34).

When you "land" in your teaching position, be it a public school, Christian school, or congregational setting as a DCE or pastor or other Christian educator, you may not encounter a large crowd, but the nature of the assembly in your classroom will be similar to what Jesus encoun-

25. Example: "You were bought with a price, therefore honor God with your bodies" (1 Cor 6:20). The Ten Commandments are introduced by the indicative, a statement of God's gracious deliverance of Israel from bondage (Exod 20:2).

tered. As sheep, we are always at risk of going astray. Although we have a Shepherd, we often live as though we do not. We too often listen to the voice of the deceiver, whose desire is not to lead us into green pastures, but into gangrenous death. This is true of you and me. It will be true, as well, of your students. Therefore, in the mold of Jesus, *teach* them. Therefore, in the pattern of Ezra, *set your heart to study the law [torah!] of the LORD, and to do it, and to teach the Good News of the kingdom: Jesus is the Christ.*

It would be easier to regard this whole matter of teaching as simply another task in life or a personal career choice, but not a calling. Then we could coast through to retirement. Then we could see our students as "clients" or "revenue resources" instead of "lambs of God." Then our teaching could be care-free instead of careful. But that is not the calling of a Christian teacher. Yours is a calling from the Lord of life. Pray that your response be like that of St. Paul, whose goal was "teaching everyone with all wisdom, that we may present everyone mature in Christ. For this I toil, struggling with all his energy that he powerfully works within me" (Col 1:28–29, ESV). Jesus is powerfully at work within you. Work faithfully for him. Be a *Christian* teacher.

3

God's Two Strategies

Part I—Teaching the Tension

Russ Moulds

This chapter locates the teaching ministry in both
the world and the church's ministry of the Gospel
(or in what are traditionally called God's two kingdoms).

"I AM THE way, and the truth, and the life. No one comes to the Father but by me" (John 14:6). It doesn't get any plainer or simpler than that. And yet we should not be surprised that God uses more than one tactic to accomplish his ultimate goal of redeeming sinners and renewing a fallen, sinful world. Given such biblical doctrines as the Trinity, the variety in creation, multiple means of grace in Word and sacraments, a dozen tribes in Israel and a dozen apostles, and his two distinct yet complementary words of Law and Gospel, we should expect the God of a lively and dynamic universe to use at least a couple of ways to be about the singular work of redemption. And given the dynamic and complex ways in which sin morphs and mutates as our situations change (consider the difficulty of maintaining a series of lies), we can expect him to be doing at least a couple of things to sustain the temporal as he simultaneously brings about the eternal.

Alas, a complex creation (he could have created a simple universe of only space and hydrogen), the tangled sins of thought, word, and deed, and God's multiple maneuvers for getting us out of that sin and together with him—all this sometimes makes for some complicated ministry decisions by those called to work with him for his ultimate aims. This chapter examines the Bible's doctrine of the two kingdoms as a basic distinction to help teachers of the church think about and "locate" our ministry and our practice. We begin with an incident not from Christian education but from public education that made national news:

Teacher Talks about Christianity: Fired

Papillion, Nebraska: Robert Ziegler, Papillion-La Vista High School math teacher, has been fired for talking about Christianity in his public high school classroom.

In a special hearing called to adjudicate the case, the Papillion-La Vista school board heard three hours of testimony, then voted unanimously to terminate Ziegler, age 24, for insubordination and unprofessional conduct.

Ziegler and school administrators both addressed the board. Ziegler said he works hard to help students by getting to know them personally and understand them. Administrators testified that Ziegler is a good instructor and that they wanted to retain him, but he refused to stop discussing religion in his classroom. This, they said, violates the constitutional separation of church and state. What's more, this deviation from the district's math curriculum violates policy.

The case came to the board as a result of some parent and student complaints about Ziegler's classroom discussions of religion. The complaint reports varied, indicating that Ziegler would talk about religion once a day or once a week for a few minutes or as long as ten minutes. Local newspaper accounts reported praise of Ziegler from other students and parents. Sophomore Ashley Fuller, 15, said about Ziegler, "He's the first teacher that made me excited to learn math."

Ziegler told the board that some of the students need God in their lives. He said that he wanted his students to have peace in their hearts and work hard. "I know that God is the only source for doing that," he said.

Papillion-La Vista High School Principal Jim Glover said that Ziegler was "a very positive force" for some students, but that his success needed to be weighed against the risk of his beliefs offending other students. "That's the very reason you have to keep this out of the classroom. It divides parents and students on what's acceptable teaching method." Zielger allowed that he "probably broke the law" by engaging in religious discussions with students but that he had to choose God's law over man's law by talking about Christianity with students. "As a teacher and Christian, He will judge me about what I've done," Ziegler said. "I'm responsible for 120 kids and what they learn."

At the announcement of the board's decision and close of the meeting, Ziegler shook hands with each board member and thanked them for their consideration. He also exchanged a brief hug with each of his administrators and thanked them as well.[1]

The Ziegler case raises many questions. Most of his students, parents, and administrators liked Rob Ziegler and appreciated his teaching and character. Was the church/state rationale used for firing him reasonable? Ziegler clearly has a sincere sense of Christian calling and discipleship. Does he have a biblically valid understanding of that calling, or should he re-think his position? Could Ziegler in good conscience alter his witness and action, continue to teach in a public school, and remain faithful? If so or if not, how would you explain this to him? What would you counsel him about his teaching in public education?

Responses and Challenges

However he might answer these questions, Mr. Ziegler is certainly thinking about the role of the Christian in the world. He is trying to put his faith into action, and we admire that faithfulness. But many—including Christians teaching in public schools and those teaching in the ministry of parish schools—aren't quite sure how to assess his action. That uncertainty stems from a set of differing and competing views among Christians about how the Christian should relate to the world. Before we clarify that set of views, first consider some different responses to the Ziegler case along with some challenges to those responses.

One response is that Mr. Ziegler has overstepped his role as a public school teacher by being outspoken about his faith. Rather than making his classroom a place of witness and testimony, he should fulfill the Second Great Commandment (see Matt 22:34–40) and serve his neighbor by being an excellent math instructor, classroom teacher, and through other conventional roles with students. In this way, he can practice Jesus' words from Matt 5:16, "Let your light so shine before men that they may see your good works and give glory to your Father who is in heaven." Many faithful Christians teach in public schools, do a good job, and are a blessing to their students through their actions and dedication, but do not violate the religious views of others in the school. In other words, given the tax-supported nature of public education and its religious diversity, the chief ministry of the Christian who teaches in public schools is to be

1. Compare the reports from the Associated Press, 12/22/2004, and *Omaha World Herald*, 12/22/2004.

a good role model, not a spokesperson for the Gospel. Mr. Ziegler should have eliminated his direct religious discourse from the classroom.

A serious challenge to this response is that our role-modeling is not a means of grace. Being a good role model refers to our works and what we do, not to what God has done for us in Christ. In terms of Law and Gospel, our being a role model for others is about a word of Law, that is, what we are to do, not to do, and how we are to live according to the laws and ordinances of God. And our works of the Law do not extend the grace and mercy of Christ to students or anyone else. Only the means of grace—God's word of Gospel and that same word in the sacraments—can convey the promises of God in Christ, create faith, and bring others into a saving relationship with God. If we are to be ambassadors of Christ (2 Cor 5:16–21), then our being a good role model is not sufficient for any Christian to conduct a ministry of the Gospel.

Another response to the case says that Mr. Ziegler is to be applauded for taking a stand based on his Christian convictions. He was respectful toward all parties involved, he shared but did not impose his views on students, he was not hostile or combative, and he cooperated completely with the administrative intervention. He lived out the Second Great Commandment and was willing to sacrifice his teaching position for the spiritual well-being of others. Mr. Ziegler conducted himself in a Christ-like manner, providing a good witness to students about the cost of discipleship in a time when they have very few examples of meaningful Christian witness—and the Greek word for witness is *martyrion*. He counted the cost of that witness and did not let the salt of the Gospel lose its taste, merely to be dismissed and thrown away. (See Luke 14:25–35.) He lost his temporal classroom but gave his students a much more important and eternal lesson.

A serious challenge to this response is that, while martyrdom is occasionally necessary, it is a last response to the world's resistance to the Gospel and to its enormous spiritual needs. Peter, who eventually gave his own witness unto death in Rome, instead counsels, "Live such good lives among the pagans that, though they accuse you of doing wrong, they may see your good deeds and glorify God on the day he visits us. Submit yourselves for the Lord's sake to every authority instituted among men: whether to the king, as the supreme authority, or to governors, who are sent by him to punish those who do wrong and to commend those who do right. For it is God's will that by doing good you should silence the ignorant talk of foolish men" (1 Pet 2:12–15). This challenge says that Mr. Ziegler would have done better to temper his explicit Christian proclamation in the classroom. Instead, he could elicit interest in spiritual topics by less direct yet effective ways such as through topics in his math instruction ("Do things that we cannot see like numbers really exist?") and non-curricular conversation with students. In this way, he could heed Jesus' injunction that in our witness we are to "be wise as serpents and innocent as doves" (Matt 10:16).

In keeping with this challenge, a third response is that Mr. Ziegler should have taken the long view. This response considers that he could do more spiritual good by adapting his witness strategy to his public school context than by precipitating a sincere but one-time-only high-profile event. Though conditions vary by school and school district, by and large public school teachers can speak to religious matters when students initiate them both in class and outside of class. Teachers cannot proselytize, but they can answer questions in a more than perfunctory way, and they can ask questions in return and recommend additional study, including the Bible. They can also direct students to other public institutions such as libraries, museums, and churches. In the long run, says this response, the Christian who teaches in the public school can do more good for more students for more years by patiently combining carefully timed and chosen language with a positive role model. As Paul says in 1 Cor 9:22, "I have become all things to all people that I might by all means save some."[2]

And one more challenge. So far we have limited the discussion of discipleship to Mr. Ziegler's teaching in a public school. But Paul reminds his readers that our entire life is vocation and discipleship when he says, "We pray that you may live a life worthy of the Lord and may please him in every way: bearing fruit in every good work, growing in the knowledge of God (Col 1:10)," and "So whether you eat or drink or whatever you do, do it all for the glory of God (1 Cor 10:31)." Mr. Ziegler has many opportunities for making his faith active in love. He could, in fact, move from individual witness in the public school to ministry within the church. He could shift from public education in the taxpayers' schools to public ministry in the congregations and their parochial schools, schools which today serve both Christian and non-Christian families and students of every spiritual variety. So, says this challenge, serving as a teacher of the church is another alternative for Mr. Ziegler's ministry in the world and for your and my ministry.

2. The Association of Christian Educators International is an organization for teachers in the public schools who are Christians. They maintain a web site at www.acei.org with an assortment of resources discussing the role of such teachers, the contents of which seem to be in the Reformed tradition with an orientation toward American evangelicalism.

Disagreements

The Ziegler case, a case about the role of the Christian in the world, is complicated by these multiple responses and challenges, all with valid yet different and sometimes conflicting alternatives. Thoughtful Christians can and do disagree about these positions. How can this be since we share a common faith in Christ? Consider two reasons.

One reason is that though Christians share a common orthodoxy (expressed, for example, in the Apostles' Creed and similar doctrinal statements), two thousand years of church history have generated a set of important yet different theological traditions that inform our individual faith in different ways. Understanding the broad strokes of those traditions can help us understand some differences in how the church has gone about its practices and witness to the Gospel. That is a large study we cannot complete here.[3] But the Ziegler case prompts us to look at one important Biblical theme in our common orthodoxy about which the church's traditions have differed regarding the Christian's life in the world.

That theme is usually called the two kingdom doctrine, and it refers to the present "kingdom" or reality of this world and the new kingdom of grace that Jesus inaugurates in his ministry, death, and resurrection. Christians hold different views about the two kingdom doctrine and how it should be applied to our life and ministry in the world. The many passages that confirm this biblical teaching include:

> Render therefore to Caesar the things that are Caesar's and to God the things that are God's. (Matt 22:21)

> Everyone must submit himself to the [world's] governing authorities, for there is no authority except that which God has established. The authorities that exist have been established by God. (Rom 13:1)

> Submit yourselves for the Lord's sake to every authority instituted among men: whether to the king, as the supreme authority, or to governors, who are sent by him to punish those who do wrong and to commend those who do right. (1 Pet 2:13–14)

> Jesus went into Galilee, proclaiming the good news of God. "The time has come," he said. "The kingdom of God is near. Repent and believe the good news." (Mark 1:14)

---

3. These traditions are often discussed in terms of Christian denominations, but themes among theological traditions now cross denominational lines and interest in denominational differences has waned among Christians in the pews. We do better to examine the themes and ideas themselves within these traditions.

> But seek first the kingdom of God, and his righteousness. (Matt 6:33)

> Jesus said, "My kingdom is not of this world. If it were, my servants would fight to prevent my arrest by the Jews. But now my kingdom is from another place." "You are a king, then!" said Pilate [the representative of the Roman Empire]. Jesus answered, "You are right in saying I am a king. In fact, for this reason I was born." (John 18:36)

> See also John 12:31, 17:14, and 1 Cor 15:24–28, among others.

A second reason that informed Christians can disagree about the Ziegler case is that even those who share the same perspective about the two kingdoms may apply it differently to different situations. As we noted at the beginning of this chapter, God is more than equal to the task of dealing with the tangled complications of sin in a dynamic, complex creation. He has provided for us different strategies for working with sin and grace, and sincere Christians will find themselves applying those strategies and tactics in different ways, depending on the needs for ministry and on which of the church's traditions informs that ministry.

Let's continue with what I think is one fairly good summary of the two kingdom doctrine and how the Christian is to be about ministry in the world. I will characterize the two kingdoms as God's two strategies through which the Christian relates to the world and will examine how the Lutheran tradition distinguishes these two strategies yet always employs both of them. Then we can compare that view with three different views held by some other Christians. Finally, we will consider how the two strategies apply to ministry for a teacher of the church.

God's Two Strategies

Heiko Oberman's biography of Luther is called *Luther: Man Between God and the Devil*. This title captures the larger context of creation, fall, and imprisonment out of which Christ must lead captive humanity (Eph 4:8). And this is the context—man between God and the devil—in which Luther always thinks (though any particular Luther document such as his two kingdom treatise, *On Secular Authority*, may not explicitly say so).

Scripture informs us of a couple of strategies God is using to free humanity captive to the devil, redeem sinners, and renew a fallen, sinful world. (God may use more than these two, but, if so, Scripture doesn't tell us, and so we shouldn't speculate too much.) One strategy is to utilize some temporal arrangements—Luther cited marriage, civil government, and the church, though not in a rigid, categorical way—generally to do three things: keep the sinful world in check to hold off chaos; promote as much common good and justice as can be had under the circumstances of the fall and the devil's hold on the world; and provide opportunities by which any person, Christian or not, can contribute to promoting to that common good and justice. Nothing about this strategy defeats the devil, saves the world, or accomplishes anyone's righteous status before God, not even the church as an organization. Note also that even though these temporal arrangements are human activities, they are actually all God's short-term good works that he does in his own hidden way. He does these things to sustain that larger context (or kingdom) for the time being so he can employ his other strategy to defeat the devil, make us righteous, and redeem creation.

God's other strategy is to broadcast some additional, peculiar news into our present larger context. The news is that, entirely without our assistance or contribution, a carpenter's life, ministry, death, and overcoming death have come and continue to come between us and the devil, undo his hold on the world, take us out of that captivity, return us to God, and put things right between heaven and earth. Like many powerful news stories, this news has a power to change people. Its particular power is that of promise and hope, hope boosted by God's own pledge standing behind the promise. God delivers this curious news in his own personal way in Jesus and continues to circulate it just as personally through Jesus' friends using word-of-mouth plus a few tactics to visualize those words (called sacraments). Even though this news flash comes through the likes of us, it is, like the first strategy, also all God's work done in his own hidden way for accomplishing his long-term aim of restoring the world and everything in it to his good graces.

So both strategies are God's strategies. Both kingdoms are God's kingdoms. God inducts us as active participants into the first, like workers given vocations; and purely passive recipients into the second, like babies being born or dead men being raised. God provides us with all the needed resources for the first: food and clothing, home and family, daily work, and all I need from day to day. For the second strategy, God imparts to us his Word from which, like a small child with no initial decision or intention, we learn to speak and then grow to speak with others. Though we as sinners and sinner-saints experience real tension between the two, God works both these strategies together in a way that for him is complementary and interactive. He does all this to bring about his aim of getting us out from between him and the devil and simply with him. And that's the two kingdom doctrine. There are other ways to express it and many angles in it to explore, but this is a fair summary, I think.[4]

While the above summary confines its description to "two strategies," the doctrine is a powerful concept that crosses all of Scripture (chiefly, Lutherans might say, as Law and Gospel). The theological literature about the two kingdoms is often difficult, using various images and not always consistently.[5] Luther's own chief writing on the two kingdoms, *On Secular Authority*, is not easy to read. It begins with the expression, "two kingdoms," but soon switches to behavioral descriptions in which the Christian both suffers injustice done to the self for the sake of the Gospel (as a chief characteristic of God's right-hand "kingdom" or "strategy") and fights ferociously in the world against injustice done to the neighbor (as a chief characteristic of God's left-hand "kingdom" or "strategy"). He then changes his two-fold language again to God's rule over the soul and our righteousness of faith through the Gospel (right-hand) and God's rule over the body and our civic righteousness in obedience to the law (left-hand).[6] Because this doctrine is so powerful, it requires both multiple images and careful rather than oversimplified treatment. The point here is that we conduct our ministry in a complex, dynamic creation fallen in sin. God's response in Christ is, of course, more than a match for sin. However, that sin still makes for some complicated conditions and decisions as we see in Christ's own ministry and in the Ziegler case.

Because it sets out the landscape for our being a Christian in the world, the two kingdom doctrine is essential for understanding the role and ministry of the teacher of the church. But the teacher must also understand how different theological traditions apply this doctrine and how they yield different views about the Christian's role in the world, such as we saw in the Ziegler case. Only then can we appreciate how Luther's two kingdom perspective so profoundly informs our teaching ministry and how teachers can assist other Christians with their left- and right-hand strategies.

4. This summary is adapted from "The Left and Right Hands of God" by Russ Moulds in *Issues in Christian Education* (Winter 2005) 39.3.

5. Theological texts and articles use such different expressions as two realms, two spheres, two governments, two swords, two perspectives, two orders, the two-fold rule of God, God's left hand and right hand, and simply justification and sanctification. The usage is often confusing and not explained well.

6. Brent W. Sockness, "Luther's Two Kingdoms Revisited: a response to Reinhold Niebuhr's criticism of Luther," *Journal of Religious Ethics* (Spring 1992). Sockness analyzes Luther's treatise, *On Secular Authority*, "to highlight the complexity of Luther's argument [regarding the two kingdoms] in a single treatise."

Relating Church and World

At Jesus' ascension, the apostles ask him if he will now restore the kingdom to Israel. They are asking him to usher in the close of the age and resolve the tension that exists between the two kingdoms. But Jesus did not and will not do so until the times and seasons fixed by the Father's authority are complete and the Gospel has done its saving work in Jerusalem, Judea, Samaria, and to the ends of the earth (Acts 1:1–11). Meanwhile the two kingdoms coexist simultaneously for us and we practice the strategies of each, yet always in tension.[7]

1. *Christ and Culture in Conflict*: Different traditions in the church have addressed this tension in different ways.[8] Some have taught that the tension is not manageable and that the two kingdoms are always in opposition, a view sometimes referred to as "Christ and culture in conflict." This view cites such texts as John 17:14, " I have given them your word and the world has hated them, for they are not of the world any more than I am of the world," and 2 Cor 6:14, 17, "Do not be yoked together with unbelievers. For what do righteousness and wickedness have in common? 'Therefore come out from them and be separate,' says the Lord." The conflict view has influenced some forms of monasticism and some Protestant separatist groups. It does not, however, represent a large number of Christians, though it is often over-emphasized in the popular media, particularly in the religion-and-science issues. The present day horse-and-buggy Amish communities provide, perhaps, a more sympathetic example.

2. *Christ Accommodating Culture*: Another tradition deals with the tension of the two strategies by trying to merge them. This approach seeks to adapt the church and its message to current cultural conditions and norms in order to keep the Gospel fresh and relevant. As various powerful cultural forces come into play through commerce, science, and politics, the church accommodates its right-hand strategy for God's coming kingdom to the prevailing themes of the present world. This "Christ accommodating culture" view says the church has merged itself with the world several times in history, such as working with Judaism in the biblical church, adjusting to the Roman Empire in the early church, and reforming the church during

---

7. The expression, "the two kingdoms doctrine," was coined by the 20th century neo-orthodox Reformed theologian, Karl Barth. He intended it as a critique and not an affirmation of the concept. See G. W. Bromiley, *An Introduction to the Theology of Karl Barth* (Edinburgh: T. & T. Clark, 1991).

8. The four descriptions that begin here are adapted from various commentaries on the book, *Christ and Culture*, by H. Richard Niebuhr (New York: Harper and Row, 1951). Niebuhr presents five different perspectives in his book.

the Renaissance. In each instance, the church has survived while the world changed. The usual concern about this approach is whether the Gospel message and God's right-hand strategy prevail or get lost in the mix. This view is often associated with what many regard as a liberal theology, a theological perspective prevalent in the nineteenth through mid-twentieth century which de-emphasized the authority of Scripture in order to conform to and (these theologians hoped) influence an increasingly secular society. A current example connected to what is called "civic religion" might be a local pastor opening a legislature or city council session with a generic prayer that omits anything to do with Christ and his name.

3. *Christ Transforming Culture*: A popular perspective among many conservative Christians is called "Christ transforming culture." This view seeks to reduce the tension between the two kingdoms by restructuring society according to biblical norms and principles. These Christians sincerely believe that the authority of God's Word—particularly his Word about the order of creation—can and should transform culture, including politics, the sciences, art, the media, family, and all things. This transformation may happen through religious revival, political influence, cultural shift, evangelism, and in other ways. Two biblical texts often invoked by this view include, "If my people, who are called by my name, will humble themselves and pray and seek my face and turn from their wicked ways, then will I hear from heaven and will forgive their sin and will heal their land," 2 Chr 7:14, and "Blessed is the nation whose God is the Lord," Ps 33:12. Based on the reports and his testimony at his hearing, Rob Ziegler in our opening case study seems to hold this "transforming" perspective. As another example, consider some religious spokespersons for the conservative side of the political spectrum such as James Dobson and Pat Robertson.

4. *Christ and Culture in Tension*: The Lutheran tradition differs from other perspectives in that it does not seek to resolve or escape the tension between the two kingdoms. Rather, this approach seeks to embrace that tension. The tension is real and problematic, as we can see in Scripture, history, and our own times. It often puts the Christian in difficult situations just as it did many biblical figures, trying to live simultaneously as a now-but-not-yet citizen of the heavenly commonwealth (Phil 3:20; Eph 2:19) while participating fully in the world God still loves (Acts 16:37; 21:39; 22:3).[9] But in the context of God's employing two strategies rather than merging or reducing one into the other, these situations of tension become the settings in which Christians craft ways to vividly exhibit the

---

9. For example, see events in Paul's ministry such as Acts 17:1–9, 18:16–34, and 25:1–12.

strife of sin in this present kingdom and the promise of grace in the new and coming kingdom.[10] God's right-hand strategy of saving sinners is not divorced from his left-hand strategy of preserving a world of sinners to be saved. The two strategies work in creative tension—that is, as God's agents, we Christians work the two strategies in creative tension—to preserve the world, keep sin in check, highlight this perpetually frustrating struggle, then announce and enact another, better hope through what God has done in Christ. Meanwhile, we also watch with anticipation for Jesus to return and resolve the tension: "He will come again with glory to judge both the living and the dead, whose kingdom will have no end" (The Apostles' Creed). An example of this tension might be our including both an American flag and a church flag in the front of the church, yet not preaching patriotism in place of the Gospel.

What Does This Mean?

God is at work through the institutions of this world, and God joins the Christian to that work.[11] In fact, that work is part of our whole calling or vocation. But we are at work with God in his left-hand strategy not for the sake of these institutions or to locate our identity or meaning in them. Rather we participate whole-heartedly and faithfully because we know this is his prior short-term strategy of preserving the world for the sake of his larger long-term strategy of saving the world. The first strategy is not indifferent to or separate from the second. It is in service to the second though this relationship is usually not directly evident.[12]

Non-Christians know nothing of this spiritual reality and presume that their life in culture is all that exists (or is somehow in league with some other deity or cosmic purpose). Biblical examples include Pharaoh, Nebuchadnezzar, and the Herod family, none of whom understood their own roles in God's greater work. By contrast, John the Baptist seemed to understand this two-fold reality when he served as both the herald of

10. The two kingdom doctrine can be rightly presented as one way to distinguish God's two words of Law and Gospel. I have found it more instructive first to discuss the doctrine as two strategies or ways in which God does his work; then explore the implications for Law and Gospel.

11. This "joining" refers to concepts such as vocation and call. We will consider these terms further in later chapters.

12. Does the left-hand kingdom have any intrinsic value of its own? One answer among others is that Genesis 1 affirms the intrinsic value of creation, but the left-hand kingdom is a temporal strategy as a means to an end. It has instrumental rather than intrinsic value as Paul seems to imply in 1 Cor 7:29 ff.

Christ and the nemesis of Herod Antipas. Today every engineer, sales clerk, crossing guard, artist, tennis pro, home maker, dentist, florist, and accountant contributes to the work of preserving God's left-hand kingdom as the context for the work of his right-hand kingdom whether they know it or not.

The biblically informed disciple who teaches in a public school or private school unrelated to the church's ministry does so as an informed agent of God's left-hand kingdom.[13] Of course, the biblically informed Christian in those schools also looks for and creates opportunities to draw others a little closer to God's right-hand kingdom of grace, that kingdom of grace which is already present in God's Word and community and is drawing ever closer as God's ultimate aim for this world. They enact this right-hand strategy using God's Word of his promises in Christ as a means of grace in their life of discipleship out in the world, usually in an informal one-to-one context. But in some of the world's left-hand settings—like public schools—our right-hand ministry is limited by the constraints of the institution.

What about Rob?

Rob Ziegler, our Christian who taught math in a public school, could certainly include public school teaching in his discipleship. But in our current society, he would not be able to use his classroom as a forum for biblical truths and as a Christ-transforming-culture program. The tension between the two kingdoms will not permit that application of strategy.

He could serve as a role model for the Second Great Commandment and include some personal witness to his faith in Christ in occasional classroom and non-classroom moments, as many Christians do. And he can certainly "live a life worthy of the calling to which you have been called" (Eph 4:1) in all his pursuits.

But his teaching will be largely limited to a left-hand strategy due to the constraints put in place by this institution of the left-hand kingdom. Public schools in our society are not communities gathered around the means of grace for God's right-hand kingdom.[14] His teaching is part of God's left-hand strategy into which Mr. Ziegler will be able to inject only

13. Home schooling, now approaching ten percent of the schooled population, may be creating another context that calls for its own two-kingdom analysis.

14. Whether the public school should be a setting for the means of grace depends on which view of Christ-and-culture we subscribe to and also how we believe a democracy in the twenty-first century should function.

occasional and limited right-hand interventions. He can, of course, create and participate in many right-hand activities through his congregation and other Christian organizations. But not through the public schools. Public schools in our society are not part of God's right-hand strategy for his kingdom of grace.[15] They do not forgive sin, create faith, deliver the sinner from death and the devil, and promise everlasting life. They are not a community entrusted with the means of grace. They cannot be managed to resolve the tension between the two kingdoms by transforming the left-hand kingdom into the right-hand kingdom. Christ alone will bring those kingdoms together in the Father's own good time (Mark 13:32).

In the mean time, we who are teachers of the church do have the community and the means for working with both God's strategies and the tension between his two kingdoms. We use our teaching opportunities in the congregation and classroom to equip God's people for the world he so loves, educate them thoroughly in his Word, document their citizenship in both kingdoms, and teach them how to serve as left- and right-hand strategists in their own discipleship. Or, as Paul puts it in Eph 4:12–13, we "equip the saints for the work of ministry, for building up the body of Christ until we all attain to the unity of the faith and the knowledge of the Son of God, to mature measure in the stature of the fullness of Christ."

We invite Mr. Ziegler and all other faithful Christians (and non-Christians who may be interested) to learn more from and about our left- and right-hand ministry of teaching, a ministry that must be both normal and peculiar. We will describe that normal-and-peculiar ministry in the next chapter.

15. A key point of the two kingdom doctrine is that cultural conditions and change complicate our ministry. In Reformation Germany, all schools were both Christian and public, and Luther constantly petitioned the princes and other public authorities to open Christian schools, support them, and pay their teachers. This public-and-parish blend never worked the way Luther hoped it would, and he never resolved the tension—nor did he expect to since, in his words, "The world is still the world."

4

God's Two Strategies

Part II—Our Peculiar Ministry

Russ Moulds

This chapter describes our two-strategy teaching as essential for
the life of the church and sets out some ways to conduct this
ministry. Here is a practical, nuts-and-bolts discussion of what
makes for *didache*, the act of teaching Christians.

I F YOU'RE reading this, you've probably been to college or are in college.
Pause a moment and recall any courses not in theology, philosophy, or
religion that seriously addressed the concerns or practice of faith. How
many of your classes in the arts and sciences included some meaningful
and at least respectful treatment of religious themes beyond any textbook
summary or perhaps the occasional example from some past or present
news event? The answer for most of us is, not many.[1]

If you attended a public university or perhaps a private college, you
may not be surprised by this answer. But the answer now also applies to
those colleges and universities that still represent or are strongly affiliated
with the church body that sponsors them. Michael Hamilton, an histo-
rian of American religion at Seattle Pacific University, says conservative
Christians rightly worry that the secularization that changed Catholic
and Protestant colleges in the twentieth century will now overtake their
schools:

1. Inclusion of religious themes or content can take different modes such as integration
(building religious content into course content), contextual (acknowledging the role of
religion in the context of the academic community), personalization (recognizing the role
of religion in the life of student or instructor), and institutional (relating the function of
the institution to its religious source such as a denomination).

This fear exists for valid reasons. Today schools connected to certain orthodox denominations—notably Southern Baptist, Missouri Synod Lutheran, and Churches of Christ—do face a real possibility of secularization. This is because these schools have always thought of their religious identity mainly in denominational terms, rather than thinking of themselves more broadly as Christian colleges. The hard truth is that the old denominational identity that has kept their schools Christian is dying. . . . [This] identity crisis has begun to show up at Missouri Synod schools . . . and Churches of Christ colleges. Fewer of their students and faculty have ties to the denomination, and those who do arrive with weaker denominational commitments. For all these schools, the problem is how to prevent their identity crisis from producing secularization.[2]

Whether the secular (from the Latin, *saeculum*, of this time or age) is a threat or an opportunity for the teacher of the church is an important part of our discussion. Five hundred years ago the University of Wittenberg, where Luther taught, faced an identity crisis from a secularization current in its day called scholasticism. Scholasticism was an intellectual movement that merged the secular philosophies of antiquity, especially that of Aristotle, with selected themes in the church's traditions. This mix contributed to and perpetuated an artificial division between sacred and secular that characterized church and society and provoked Luther and the other Reformers to action. They rejected scholasticism. Then, beginning at Wittenberg, they demolished the barriers between God's kingdom of creation and his kingdom of grace and, while sustaining both, brought the two into relation with each other. Where there had been a two-tiered religious hierarchy with the clergy and church leaders as the "real" Christians and all others as second-class Christians, the Reformation re-discovered the biblical content of the two kingdom doctrine, relocated all Christians into both kingdoms, and inducted all Christians into both of God's strategies.[3]

2. "A Higher Education" by Michael S. Hamilton at *ChristianityToday.com* (May 27, 2005) now archived at http://www.christianitytoday.com/ct/2005/20.30.html. Hamilton reviews several books on the state of Christian higher education and proposes some ways to sustain an authentic Christian college identity.

Tom Christenson critiques the argument that secularism is a threat to Lutheran higher education. He does so on the basis of the doctrine of vocation and the Christian's call into the world, not away from it. See his book, *The Gift and Task of Lutheran Higher Education* (Minneapolis: Augsburg Fortress, 2004), and his article, "Brief Comments on 'Our Calling in Education: A First Draft of a Social Statement,'" in the *Journal of Lutheran Ethics*, July, 2006 (www.elca.org/jle).

3. For further context of these events see *Luther's World of Thought* by Heinrich Bornkamm (St. Louis: Concordia Publishing House, 1958), and *The Structure of Lutheranism*,

For Wittenberg and other universities of the Reformation, the result was a revision of their entire curriculum around the Reformation's central insights about the Gospel, a revision that emphasized the importance to the Reformation of all academic programs and disciplines. The new curriculum reorganized theological instruction for pastors and teachers but also included it in the other professions of law and medicine, and in the colleges of arts and sciences—and kept them all together in a mutually informing way. Marilyn Harran in her book, *Martin Luther: Learning for Life*, describes the curriculum revision:

> Concerns for building leaders in church and state led Luther to turn to the reform of the universities. . . . Luther underscored the importance of the universities. They educate the leaders of society, those who become the jurists, educators, and pastors of tomorrow. Thus, Luther proclaimed that "there is no work more worthy of pope or emperor than a thorough reform of the universities. And on the other hand, nothing could be more devilish or disastrous than unreformed universities."
>
> As the foremost authority and heart of the curriculum, Scripture was at the center of Luther's vision of the university. Scripture is the core of the curriculum, not only in theology but in the arts faculty as well.
>
> The influence of educated people extends to the whole world. Without educated people performing their spiritual and secular duties, all of society will crumble for "when the theologians disappear, God's Word also disappears and nothing but heathen remain, indeed, nothing but devils. When the jurists disappear, then the law disappears, and peace with it, and nothing but robbery, murder, crime, and violence remain." In the midst of such chaos, not even the most dedicated businessman . . . will be able to maintain his position—"what earnings and profits the businessman will have when peace is gone, I shall let his ledger tell him."[4]

The schools and universities of the Reformation were not Bible colleges.[5] Scripture did not dictate their course content—a notion entirely

by Werner Elert (St. Louis: Concordia Publishing House, 1962).

4. From *Martin Luther: Learning for Life*, by Marilyn Harran (Concordia Publishing House, 1997) 168, 196. Harron describes the partnership of Martin Luther and his colleague, Philip Melancthon, as they reform the teaching ministry in theology and the arts and sciences at the University of Wittenberg.

5. The term "Bible college" generally refers to two-to-four year post-secondary schools associated with the Fundamentalist movement of the twentieth century whose curriculum is usually a combination of Bible study courses and general education courses in English

foreign to their understanding of the Bible as God's word of Law and Gospel for sinners. They rejected scholaticisim, but they did not abandon the secular. Rather, they designed curriculum in which the Scriptures actively informed the purpose of education and that course of study. These university teachers of the church had the essential task of preparing Christians thoroughly educated for life and service with both God's left- and right-hand strategies because the larger purpose of God's redeeming work depends on the prior purpose of sustaining a sin-plagued world of sinners in need of redemption. This purpose was not merely intuitive or passively "understood" by faculty and students. It was deliberately designed into the curriculum, articulated, and regularly debated in class and by the faculty.[6] The stakes were far too high to take the purpose of education for granted, for, in their estimation, it was the Reformation and the Gospel that were at stake.

Today, despite all our polished mission and visions statements, we may ask, Have we largely lost this both/and purpose for our education? It may not be overstatement to say that in the congregations, we proclaim sermons and direct Christian education but without serious attention to the role of the Christian in the world. And in our schools and universities, we deliver instruction in the subject areas, the liberal arts, and professional programs but without meaningful connection to God's Word in the life of that Christian. If so (and I think too much so), the expression that applies here to our teaching in both congregation and school is "disconnect."[7]

In the previous chapter we examined God's two strategies for accomplishing his temporal and eternal purposes for sinners and how those strategies work in tension with each other. In this chapter we consider how connecting the two strategies makes our teaching peculiar. We can then better understand why our two-kingdom education is not easy to conduct but is critical for the life of the church and the world. Some clarifications will assist our understanding.

communication and history. Many Bible colleges of this period have now developed into four-year accredited institutions in the liberal arts while retaining much of their Bible curriculum.

6. Harran explains that these disputations and declamations "became occasions for students to debate the real issues of the day and to gain skill in presenting their arguments eloquently. For pastors and teachers who would be caught in the increasing whirlwind of religious dissension such skill was absolutely essential" (Harran, 245).

7. I have many colleagues in congregations, schools, and university classrooms whose ministry makes this paragraph hyperbole. Yet the concern Hamilton expresses in this chapter's opening citation prompts many of these same colleagues to ponder the condition of our Christian identity and spiritual effectiveness.

The Left and Right Hands of Public Ministry

Our first clarification has to do with church workers and the two kingdoms. The Christian who serves in the public ministry of the church is a participant in both God's left-hand and right-hand strategies. Let's first consider the right-hand strategy. God has entrusted the church with the means of grace, those right-hand means of the proclaimed Gospel and sacraments by which sinners are inducted and sustained in God's eternal kingdom. Of course, all Christians extend these means (chiefly the verbal good news of the Gospel) to others personally and informally in all our life activities. Those among us who conduct the public ministry of those means of grace as the church's pastors, directors of Christian education, teachers, and other called servants apply these right-hand means in a public way through the sacraments, preaching, and instruction of God's Word.

But our public ministry also includes a ministry of God's left-hand strategy. When a pastor officiates at a wedding, meets with a city official about a building campaign, or shovels snow off the sidewalk before worship, that pastor serves also as a left-hand strategist. None of these activities forgives sins or creates faith (though the Gospel of the right-hand kingdom can potentially and should be shared in many left-hand activities), but all of them maintain the context for God's larger and eternal aims. When a teacher of the church learns a biblical language, coaches a sport, or presents a lesson on Reformation history, that teacher serves as a left-hand strategist. These teaching activities are in service to God's ultimate right-hand aims, though only his right-hand strategies with the means of grace—chiefly the Word integrated into those left-hand activities—will actually bring about those purposes. Our life as God's person is always the life of both a left- and right-hand strategist, always understanding that both are necessary but that the left-hand work is done for the sake of the right-hand work.

Separate Checks, Please?

Some Lutheran essayists have staked out a strong (too strong, I will argue in a moment) dualistic position on the two kingdoms, seeking to keep them separate from each other. We often see this compartmentalized position in brief treatments of the two kingdom doctrine. For example, in church-and-state matters, we don't want the civil government telling the church what it can preach, and we don't want the church collecting taxes in the offering plate. Both realms or governments function best with a high wall of separation, according to this view. The science-and-religion debates include a similar view by which science operates with a methodological naturalism that doesn't test for miracles and religion includes a supernaturalistic theism that presumes miracles. Both may sit at the same table and be served by the same waiter, but let's have separate checks, please.[8]

This dualistic position is also often applied to education in this way. If I prepare for a career in business or the trades or a profession, that choice and action may be influenced by God's love for me in Christ, motivating me to serve my neighbor in one of these ways. But that choice and action cannot forgive my sin, commend me to God, or assist me in getting to heaven. My own course of action cannot justify me before God since my only justification is Christ and him crucified. It's best then to avoid the danger of self-justification and contain the matters of our works in the left-hand kingdom and the matters of salvation in the right-hand kingdom in order to keep the Gospel as the Gospel. In fact, in this view, the Gospel itself gives us the freedom and liberty to make this compartmentalization without incurring any spiritual danger of falling afoul of God.

This view has a valid concern. It rightly argues that the Gospel unilaterally secures our well-being with God, freeing us for educational and occupational pursuits without having to use these pursuits to please or placate God.[9] Education and occupation are about our works in the world, the left-hand kingdom, and this position points out the great danger of us sinners mixing our efforts into God's saving Word and works. The old Eve and Adam always prefer works righteousness to God's grace. Therefore this view recommends we keep the kingdoms and their strategies apart except as they co-exist in the interior, personal, spiritual life of the individual justified-and-sanctified Christian. This position is not quite the Christ-and-culture-in-conflict model (summarized in the previous essay), but it certainly compartmentalizes the two kingdoms with no overlap or intersection between them and no relationship between the two strategies.

8. This compartmentalist view is only one of several models for assessing Christ-and-culture issues with the two kingdom doctrine. For several perspectives on Christ and culture, see *Christ and Culture in Dialogue* edited by Angus Menuge (St. Louis: Concordia Publishing House, 1999). For further discussion on science-and-religion, see *Science & Christianity: Four Views*, edited by Richard F. Carlson (Downers Grove, IL: Intervarsity, 2000). For an introduction and additional references to church-and-state issues, see *Issues in Christian Education*, 39.3 (Winter 2005), "Religious Expression in the Public Square." See also assorted articles online in the *Journal of Lutheran Ethics* at www.jle.org.

9. What's more, pursuing a church work occupation will not commend us to God any more than pursuing a non-church work occupation since both are part of God's two-strategy work on behalf of sinners. We will consider this further in chapters on the priesthood of all believers and vocation.

Creative Tension

But this compartmentalist position overreaches its proper concern. The Bible that teaches *sola fides* and *sola gratia* is the same Bible that teaches the incarnation and the sacraments. In the birth of Christ, God enacts a right-hand campaign that invades the left-hand kingdom. In the sacraments, God employs ordinary elements of this world–water, bread, and wine—to effect the promises and outcomes of the right-hand kingdom. In the flood, the exodus, the exile, the crucifixion, and the Apostles' ministries, we see God's right-hand strategy (choose your preferred word for incursion here) penetrating, intersecting, permeating, infusing, infecting, and invading the left-hand realm. Scripture is full of such instances. The Bible is a narrative of God's intercepting selected "instances" in this world and enlisting them in service to his right-hand aims, most importantly in Christ.

The left- and right-hand kingdoms are not the same kingdoms, and God's strategies with each are not the same strategies. But they are not compartmentalized from each other here in the so-called "real world," as though they exist together only in the mind of God or the personal interior faith of the individual Christian. For the time being, the right continues to intrude on the left in public and conspicuous ways, just as we see in so many Biblical examples. This intrusion generates tension—call it a creative tension—between the two strategies. Only at the close of the age will that tension be resolved and the right- and left-hand realms be united in God's new heaven and earth (Eph 1:3–10, 1 Cor 15:20–28, Rev 21:1–4). Meanwhile, what we do now in our ministry with this tension is a precursor or foretaste of what God will do finally and completely in the risen and returning Christ.

Perhaps we can say that this tension *is* our ministry, as described in Jesus' high-priestly prayer: "My prayer is not that you take them out of the world but that you protect them from the evil one. They are not of the world, even as I am not of it. Sanctify them by the truth; your word is truth. As you sent me into the world, I have sent them into the world" (John 17:15–18). Jesus does not pray that this tension would be resolved for us. He sends us forthright into the domain of the evil one with all the tension that implies. He does not say that our protection comes from retreating from the world, or accommodating it, or transforming it, or in some other way resolving the tension. He says our means for being his person in the world is his Word, and as John's Gospel continues, Jesus next exhibits that Word for us on the cross where all the tension of Law and Gospel comes together.

As often as we may hear and sound the byte of "in the world, not of the world," we teachers of the church have not much developed content and delivery for putting this tension into our own practice and helping our fellow redeemed recognize it and live it.

Normal and Peculiar

This both/and (rather than a compartmentalized either/or) of God's two strategies makes for a ministry that is both normal and peculiar. The Gospel frees us from relying on our activity in the world for our well-being with God (Did the school Christmas program turn out well? Have I had enough winning basketball seasons? Do I really know how to teach organic chemistry yet?) and propels us into Jesus' Great Commission ministry to the world (Matt 28:19–10). The two-strategy Christian looks pretty normal in most ways, being about the usual roles, jobs, and activities that we find in the world. But this same Gospel further assures us that nothing can separate us from the love of God in Christ. (See Paul's powerful testimony in Rom 8:31–39.) So this Gospel also empowers us, for the sake of our neighbor's temporal and eternal well-being, to take risks and make decisions that do not merely conform to the usual activities and expectations of this world (Rom 12:1–8). And because our neighbor's temporal and spiritual condition is always at risk from the devil, the world, and the sinful self, sometimes in complicated ways, we who are assured and secure in the Gospel will sometimes for the sake of our neighbor decide and act in ways that seem peculiar to others.[10]

For the most part our ministry as a teacher of the church employs practices that are typical of the congregational or classroom role to which we are called. We conduct ourselves within the expectations of that role, and our work and life look conventional, as we would expect them to look in the context of Luther's meaning for the First Article of the Apostles' Creed: "God provides me with food and clothing, home and family, daily work, and all I need from day to day." And God's right-hand strategy of the Gospel finds its way into this conventional pattern through our

---

10. Luther offers some interesting discussion about the need for Christian behavior that is sometimes troubling and offensive. See his counsel on when to spite the princes in his *Treatise on Secular Authority*. See also the closing pages to his *Treatise on Christian Liberty* where, regarding legalists who seek to define our Christian life by their rule-making, Luther says the Christian "must resist, do the very opposite, and offend them boldly." (At what point in their educational development shall we teach this to our students? Will their parents, spouses, pastors, and other teachers appreciate it?)

devotions, Sunday worship, chapel, Bible study, conversation, and daily forbearance with each other. Still fairly normal.

But as we considered in the previous chapter, a world plunged in sin is messy and can get complicated. Then the conventional doesn't always work so well. Or sometimes an event presents itself or is needed to highlight profoundly the difference between the left-hand and right-hand kingdoms, things visible and invisible, things now and things to come.[11]

Figure 4.1 God's Two Kingdoms and Strategies For the Sake of the Gospel

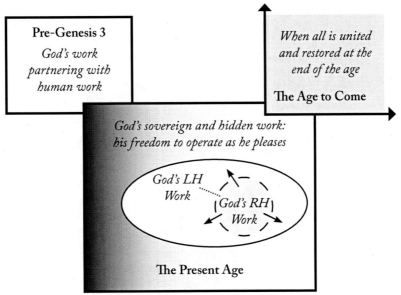

God's two strategies in the present age

Left hand: temporary, penultimate, but good and useful.

Right hand: eternal, ultimate, but not yet fully completed.

OUR MESSY GOSPEL MINISTRY: The left- and right-hand strategies are not the same works, but they are not isolated from each other. As active agents of both God's strategies, we must judge and decide how much the left hand may influence the right hand (too much and the Gospel is eclipsed), and how much the right hand intrudes on the left (we don't want theo-

---

11. I suspect Rob Ziegler, our public school math teacher in the previous chapter, detected this need for his students, and that takes us back to our discussion of responses and challenges to his action.

cracy where sinners—even sinner-saints—presume to be God's viceroys). What this ministry lacks in Pharisaic precision, it makes up for by keeping the left hand and right hand in tension in order to feature and distinguish the Gospel.

Figure 4.2 Four Ways to Misapprehend the Left- and Right-Hand Strategies

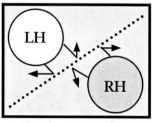

Kingdoms in conflict (tends toward double predestination)

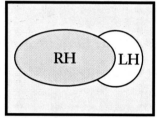

The right hand seeking to transform the left-hand kingdom (tends toward double predestination)

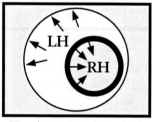

Kingdoms compartmental-ized (tends toward double predestination)

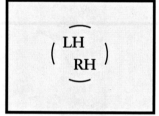

Kingdoms accommodated— no boundaries (tends toward universalism)

A TIDY LAW ORIENTATION: Each of these ways to relate the left- and right-hand kingdoms tends to rely on and over-compensate with God's Word of Law. In an effort to define precisely, maintain, contain, reduce, erase, or otherwise manage the boundaries, these efforts look to the Law to resolve the tension between the two kingdoms rather than employing that tension to highlight the Gospel which alone effects real change.

Driving on the Wrong Side

The Bible includes many examples of God's right-hand saving strategy crossing into his left-hand maintenance-of-this-world strategy, sometimes in peculiar ways. Perhaps the most extreme example is the almighty and infinite Lord of the universe born as a human infant in an animal stall. We have also already mentioned baptism and communion. Leviticus 25 describes the sabbath year in which no crops were planted and the jubilee year in which debt and servitude obligations were cancelled, both ways of enacting Israel's trust in Yahweh's promises. In Ezra 9–10, Ezra commands the divorce of Jewish men from non-Jewish wives, a drastic and controversial command that disturbs our modern sensibilities. When Jesus confronts the demons, Legion, in Mark 5, he dismisses them into the swine, and the herdsmen incur a financial loss of 2,000 head of livestock. The Gospel can be expensive and inconvenient even for bystanders. In the next chapter of Mark, John the Baptist makes the impolitic move of publicly condemning King Herod for taking his brother's wife, Herodias, as his own. Jesus interferes with the usual course of life and death in John 11 when he calls Lazarus forth from the grave and creates lots of negative attention (John 11:45–57). In Matt 17:26, Jesus instructs Peter that he is free from paying taxes. Then in the next verse, he addresses the tension he has created for Peter by supernaturally providing for the tax. Paul refuses to accept any salary or material support from his congregation in Corinth, telling them in 1 Cor 9 that in order to exhibit the Gospel more clearly, he will not practice Jesus' own command that those who proclaim the Gospel should get their living by the Gospel.

What are we to make of these and other curious episodes when God, so to speak, pulls out of the proper lane and starts driving down the wrong side of the street? Most of our own conduct as left- and right-hand strategists is not as unusual or dramatic as these examples. Most of the time, we generally follow the Ten Commandments and live under God's grace when we do fall short of the Law. But sometimes, as we see in these biblical episodes, life's sinful circumstances amplify the tension between the two kingdoms, giving opportunity for a profound setup for the Gospel and demonstration of God's grace. Or we deliberately amplify the tension because we see an opportunity to feature effectively the power and promise of the Gospel. In these instances, our ministry does not conform to the normal expectations of the left-hand kingdom but instead becomes distinctly peculiar and demonstrative of the right-hand kingdom. Before we consider some applications for common teaching circumstances, we can note some principles and guidelines for doing this left-hand and right-hand ministry.

Some Principles and Guidelines

First, as discussed above, most of our ministry most of the time should look pretty conventional. We conduct our teaching tasks and responsibilities in the congregation and classroom in ways that conform to this world. We plan curriculum, meet with groups, teach math facts, prepare for Confirmation Sunday, coach basketball, teach the new members' class, go to professional conferences, do lunch duty, and all those other things that our offices require of us.

But all our conventional activities are put in check by 1 Cor 7:29 where Paul writes, "I mean, brothers, that the time is short. From now on those who have wives should live as if they had none; those who mourn, as if they did not; those who are happy, as if they were not; those who buy something, as if it were not theirs to keep; those who use the things of the world, as if not engrossed in them. For this world in its present form is passing away." Ultimately, our activities in this world don't count except insofar as they serve God's larger outcomes.[12]

This is a strange and peculiar conviction to sustain. It has no support or affirmation outside of Scripture, and all our other life sources tell us otherwise: that our plans, activities, and aspirations are valuable for their own sake. Yet in light of the Gospel, these other sources are nonsense: "For whoever wants to save his life will lose it, but whoever loses his life for me and for the gospel will save it. What good is it for a man to gain the whole world, yet forfeit his soul?" (Mark 8:35–36).

Because all the other sources that surround us refer us only to the things of this world, we who are teachers of the church provide additional content to our usual teaching. This content exploits life's events, conditions, and incidents where the Law does its work in order to highlight God's other Word of Gospel that he would have prevail for sinners: "Go and learn what this means—'I desire mercy, not sacrifice'" (Matt 9:13).[13] Luther points out that in life, "The Law is our constant companion, but

---

12. Some will consider this an overstatement. Certainly, Scripture does not denigrate our service to neighbor and world. Instead, Scripture promotes it and even demands it under the Law, particularly in terms of justice, a powerful theme in the Torah, the prophets, the Gospels, and Paul's letters. God's Word is not life- or world-denying. But ultimately, it locates life- and world-affirming values in God's own character and his eschatological outcomes. My concern is that we often miss Scripture's (and Luther's) larger perspective.

13. Jesus' ministry in all four Gospels can be profitably read using this Law-Gospel hermeneutic principle. God clearly desires both mercy and sacrifice. But he just as clearly sets a priority of importance for these two words, a priority affirmed in both the Old and New Testaments. See Matt 12:7, Hos 6:6, and Mic 6:6–8.

the Gospel is a rare visitor to our hearts." We deliver this additional content—the content that uses life's events in addition to our usual textbooks and curriculum—in ways in which the Gospel predominates. As Charles Blanco, one of our essayists in this book, puts it, we over-compensate with the Gospel because, as Luther puts it, the Gospel is a rare visitor to our hearts, and, as we noted above, all our other sources in life are directing us only to the present form of this world even though it is passing away,

We need not saturate our ministry with these sorts of life lessons. Most of the time, we get along pretty well operating within the structure and rules of our community and office of teacher. We have no formula for when to inject one of these additional lessons. When to do so is a matter of good judgment and experience. The teacher is a right- and left-hand strategist, and the strategist calls the shot and makes the difference. And sometimes makes mistakes.

Another way to describe our two-strategy teaching is to say that we operate with both Law and Gospel. C. F. W. Walther was a Lutheran theologian who gave much thought to applying the Gospel to the lives of sinners. He begins his book, *The Proper Distinction Between Law and Gospel*, by alerting us that learning to distinguish and apply Law and Gospel is the most difficult skill for Christian teachers, a skill taught only by the Holy Spirit in the school of experience.[14] So the new teacher will make many mistakes as a Law-and-Gospel, left- and right-hand strategist. Since this sort of teaching is not the usual pedagogy and lesson-planning but is, instead, our peculiar teaching, we will generally do it badly at first in order to learn to do it well (we will consider two case examples at the end of this chapter).

Because properly distinguishing and applying Law and Gospel goes beyond the normal left-hand strategy and structure of pedagogy, the tension between the two kingdoms is not only our opportunity but also our obstacle. This highest skill of Christian teaching is difficult to master. We have no recipe. Acquiring it through the school of experience can be discouraging and frustrating (even as it is rewarding when we see the Gospel change the life of one in our care). And we tend more often to get it wrong before we more often get it right. We must, then, proceed humbly on God's promise and assurance rather than relying on our self-confidence. Paul encouraged the Corinthian Christians in this way: "Such confidence as this is ours through Christ before God. Not that we are competent in

14. See C. F. W. Walther's Thesis III in any translation of *The Proper Distinction Between Law and Gospel*, for example, *Law and Gospel*, tr. Herbert J. A. Bouman (St. Louis: Concordia Publishing House, 1981) 32.

ourselves to claim anything for ourselves, but our competence comes from God. He has made us competent as ministers of a new covenant—not of the letter but of the Spirit; for the letter kills, but the Spirit gives life" (2 Cor 3:5–6).

Not Enough Right-Hand Turns

I have said that as a ministry of both God's left- and right-hand strategies, our teaching should look both normal and peculiar. My critique of Lutheran education in the congregation and in the classroom at all levels is that it looks pretty normal without the peculiar. Our teaching and administration is pedestrian, plodding along after the same trends and fads that characterize secular education. Teaching the content of the kingdom of this world is definitely part of our left-hand strategy. We also gain many valuable insights and techniques from the left-hand kingdom. That kingdom is also God's kingdom which, although compromised by sin, retains the goodness of his created gifts. Our left-hand ministry includes all of temporal value that the kingdom and powers of this world have to offer, which is much. But a glance in the rearview mirror indicates that we don't seem to make many right-hand turns.

Our problem lies not with employing our left-hand strategy but with neglecting our right-hand strategy—or minimizing it to stereotypic and formulaic content in devotions, religion lessons, and chapels—and, by default, letting the left-hand strategy predominate. The assumption seems to be that if we keep rerunning our devotions, worksheets, and chapel talks (or some equivalent for parish or college education), then we have done our bit for the coming kingdom and we can get back to the real business of educating for this world.

But Paul identifies a different outlook and set of tactics for his right-hand strategy:

> For though I am free from all men, I have made myself a slave to all, that I might win the more. To the Jews, I became as a Jew in order to win Jews. To those under the law, I became as one under the law—though not myself being under the law—that I might win those under the law. To those outside the law, I became as one outside the law—not being without law toward God but under the law of Christ—that I might win those outside the law. To the weak I became weak that I might win the weak. I have become all things to all men that I might by all means save some. I do it all for the sake of the Gospel, that I may share in its blessings. (1 Cor 9:19–23)

Now, Paul is no other-worldly idealist, out of touch with "the way things work" in this world. He knows how the world's institutions and systems operate, and he knows how to use them, though he also knows they are all passing away. Because he knows that souls will pass away with them—those under the law, those outside the law, the weak, and all the rest—he knows how to recalculate his left- and right-hand strategies as needed in order to accomplish the larger aims of the right-hand kingdom of Jesus, who says, "Heaven and earth will pass away, but my words will not pass away" (Matt 24:35). As we see in the Book of Acts and his letters, Paul uses every sort of practice (and some are downright wily!) that he might by all means save some.[15]

Are These Christian Practices?

In chapter 3 we surveyed the two kingdoms, the two strategies God uses in these kingdoms, and the importance of sustaining the tension between the two for the Christian in the world. In this chapter we have considered why that tension generates a ministry that is both conventional and peculiar for the teacher of the church. But what does all this look like in a teaching ministry? To gather these themes together for application, we can look first at several normal activities in teaching. Then we can examine two cases of using a left-hand strategy to set up a right-hand strategy.

To help participants in courses and conferences understand this peculiar ministry, I begin by asking the trick question of whether these common teaching practices are Christian practices:

- honor roll/dean's list
- class elections
- memorizing the catechism
- *Book-It* (the Pizza Hut reading program)
- vying for valedictorian
- eligibility for participating in retreats or youth gatherings
- tracking (blue readers, red readers, green readers, etc.)
- athletic cuts
- detention, suspension, expulsion
- honors and awards assemblies
- competing for first chair clarinet
- token systems

15. See for example Paul's letter to Philemon, Acts 23:1–10, 1 Cor 5, and 2 Cor 2:5–11. See also Jesus' parable of the unrighteous steward in Luke 16:1–9.

In these presentations, the discussion escalates as participants at first wonder why I would even ask about such normal practices, but then begin to notice how many of these practices promote works righteousness.[16] Others point out that mediocrity does not honor God and that our stewardship includes the excellence these practices encourage. Yet some note that several of these practices inculcate sinful pride and put students in opposition with each other, recalling that Scripture says we should serve our neighbor and "in humility count others better than yourself." (See Phil 2:1–11 and Luke 14:1–24.) Some also note that these practices have little to do with teaching about God's right-hand kingdom of grace, while others respond that disciples need to learn to be as wise as serpents, not just innocent as doves (Matt 10:16) and that the Master wishes to say, "Well done, good and faithful servant" (Matt 25:21). The exchange accesses not just this or that proof text but several Biblical themes and contexts of Law and Gospel.

The conversation generally follows a pattern of mild curiosity, engaged discussion, shifting points of view, then puzzlement that many of the practices can be biblically criticized or defended. Participants are frustrated that some correct position is not obvious, especially since we so commonly and readily accept these practices. They encounter the tension.

Only when I next ask them to analyze these practices in terms of God's two strategies are they able to locate them in God's left-hand kingdom. They then realize these practices—depending on how they are integrated into a spiritual learning community—may be appropriate penultimate activities for maintaining a fallen creation and keeping sin in check but are not to be regarded as ultimately important or as the real purpose of their teaching ministry. They also recognize that the world's educational institutions already include these normal practices, and that if these are our main or only strategy, then we don't have much reason to exist, merely duplicating what the world can already do. And now they can further understand that while we certainly have a left-hand ministry, we are about much more than the left-hand kingdom's aims and goals, and that the church's right-hand teaching ministry will sometimes use these left-hand practices in peculiar ways to advance its right-hand strategy for the Gospel of God's right-hand kingdom.[17]

16. Luther distinguishes two genuine forms of righteousness, one by works and one by faith. See for example his sermon, "Two Kinds of Righteousness," and his opening discussion in his *Commentary on Galatians*.

17. Again, a standard Law-and-Gospel analysis is useful for exploring these choices and practices. I recommend a reading or re-reading of Walther's *Law and Gospel* as a practical

When we ask how we might enlist a left-hand practice as part of a right-hand strategy, we are tempted to look for a formula or program for doing this. But as we said earlier, we have no formula and to ask for one is to ask for another law—which leaves us in the left-hand strategy and kingdom. Consider how Jesus' ministry is non-formulaic and appears at first to be inconsistent. Jesus addresses Nicodemus, the woman at the well, the rich young ruler, the woman taken in adultery, the ten lepers, and Zacchaeus very differently. Some get Law, some Gospel. Some he gives tasks, others he blesses and sends home. Consider how Paul's ministry appears to be inconsistent. He circumcises Timothy but refuses to circumcise Titus. In Jesus' and Paul's ministries, their responses to situations vary, but their aim is consistent: "to seek and to save the lost," "that I might by all means save some," and "all for the sake of the Gospel."

We, too, are God's left-hand and right-hand strategists, and our tactics and responses vary depending on the needs of our ministry. Sometimes our efforts are for the individual, sometimes for the group. We consider age and personal development, and the person's or group's spiritual formation and relationship with God. But always in our normal activities and opportunities, we weigh our intervention strategy according to what peculiar decision and action (if any) may best draw them into or further into the right-hand kingdom of grace. The teachers of the church are always asking, How can we use our left-hand circumstances to set up an intersection with the coming right-hand kingdom of God so that others may better see God's great goodness for us in Christ?

Two Illustrations

Our space is limited. Two strategy examples will have to do as illustrations. Both are descriptive, not prescriptive. The first is brief, transparent, and non-controversial. My colleague, Janell Uffelman, is a literacy expert who teaches undergraduate and graduate courses in literacy, works with English-as-a-second-language programs, and organizes major literacy festivals that are famously successful. At first glance her efforts appear to be the work of the left-hand kingdom and, of course, they are. Literacy education is not itself a means of grace, and many sinners have entered God's coming kingdom without benefit of reading or writing. She does not structure overt faith integration curriculum or experiences into her work. But Uffelman is a wise strategist who intentionally uses literacy as one way to prepare others for reading God's Word which is a means of

study for the teacher of the church.

grace. Though her literacy festivals include no explicit religious content, they help establish and enhance her already manifest credibility. Her graduate classes give her many opportunities to share her faith on a personal basis with small professional groups of peers who are already impressed by her expertise. Her undergraduate classes then become her opportunity to acquaint and train new teachers not only for literacy education but in how to use literacy to advance God's right-hand kingdom. Uffelman's is a good teaching example of normal and peculiar together.

The second example is a controversial grading policy from my own ministry that illustrates the freedom and risks for setting up an encounter with Law and Gospel, in this case with high school students. (I sometimes use a modified form in college classes.) Consider its merits and difficulties.

Unlike some teachers, I give, collect, and immediately grade and return my assignments in a systematic way. I am not a harsh grader nor am I a perfect grader, but I am timely and consistent. By and large, students agree my assignments are not busy work but are meaningful, and are reasonably graded, perhaps a bit on the easy side.

I sometimes use a "cutthroat" grading policy. It is especially effective with middle school and early high school students. The "law of the covenant" (cf. Deuteronomy) is that I do a good job preparing assignments and returning them in a timely way, and the student does a good job completing them and submitting them in a timely way. All is just and fair under the law. But if a student does not turn in an assignment, all grading stops until that assignment is reasonably completed and submitted. This means if the student skips even one assignment yet submits the next and all later assignments, I don't grade those assignments. I put them in safe storage and ignore them, and I enter no further grades (including tests, reports, and projects) in the grade book until the missing assignment is submitted. When and where the student stops working, I stop grading. When the student continues where the student left off, I then continue with the grading. And I don't bother about late penalties under this system since additional penalties are not useful or needed with this policy. The system is already ruthlessly just—and cutthroat. You can see where this is going. (Newer teachers should not use this policy.)

For most students, the cutthroat policy poses no problems. I document it and explain it to students and parents at the beginning of the year. I post a running grade book record (names are coded) so all can see exactly where they stand. Most students who miss an assignment promptly make it up and re-start their grade where they left off. Simple. The policy promotes thorough and timely effort, accountability, responsibility, paced learning, and higher grades. It makes a positive rather than negative difference for most students.

But it can make the biggest difference for those students who remain oblivious to the policy or believe that somehow they are exempt. For them the policy can be apocalyptic. A few students miss several assignments and scramble yet fail to make them up in time; or they simply despair. Either way, they don't pass that marking period, and then we get to talk about their beliefs and decisions—a very important discussion. A few students miss a few assignments, wait to catch them up at the end of the marking period, and get their grade. This choice can work, but it is dangerous. Consider the kid who plays fast and loose with the policy but has to leave town unexpectedly when his grandfather dies suddenly. He did not get an old assignment in, his grade stopped early in the marking period, and he has a failing grade. This also creates the opportunity for useful discussion.

To those who then protest that the policy is not fair, I show them the policy in the course documentation along with James 2:10, "Whoever keeps the whole law but fails in one point has become guilty of all of it," and Jesus' teaching in Matt 24:45–51 about faithful and unfaithful servants at the close of the age. The problem with the policy is not that it is unfair. The problem is that it is only fair. The policy is cutthroat. It has no mercy. But, of course, policies don't have mercy. Ministers of the Gospel and teachers of the church have mercy. They may or may not exercise it, depending on the spiritual condition and needs of the sinner.

The school year has four marking periods for the student to establish a course grade, and the end of one marking period is not judgment day. But it looks a little like it. The cutthroat policy gives me, a teacher of the church, a chance to help student and parent reflect on life, sin, judgment, and grace. With those few students who "violate" it, the policy usually stands, and I don't alter it, no matter whether it's a "good" kid or not. It stands especially firm for those students who insist they deserve special consideration. But most students understand what's happened, take ownership for their choices, and we continue on together, two sinners in good company. (In case you're wondering, students say my classes are usually pretty lively and enjoyable. I hope so.)

But I am also Jesus' agent, chiefly of grace (though not cheap grace). And in some cases, perhaps when a grandparent dies or illness sets in and when the student knows that he is desperately lost, then I sweep away the law just as Christ on the cross has carried away the curse of the law for us. And maybe, with some mutual Christian conversation and consolation, the student and parent get a glimpse of God's mercy. It's not a perfect parallel. And it's not really my mercy since all grace ultimately comes from God, and I am merely the agent. It's certainly not fair. But "judgment is without mercy to one who has shown no mercy; and mercy triumphs over judgment (James 2:13). This, in the end, is what the teacher of the church strives to teach.[18]

Bringing Strategy and Practice Together

The reader can return to our earlier list of practices and consider ways in which some of these left-handed strategies can be used to set up our right-hand strategy. Should we bestow honors and awards at the graduation of university students? Or have we educated them well enough for both kingdoms that such a practice would be unnecessary and incongruent with their spiritual development, and even a little demeaning? Is the rite of confirmation also a confirmation of the young Christian's temporary citizenship in this world? How might we practice tracking and grouping with elementary school children such that it does not foster a sinful form of pride, partisanship, and division among God's children? Do the adults in our congregational Bible classes need more Biblical literacy? Or do they need more linkage to the headlines in this morning's newspaper?

Our left- and right-hand strategies will vary depending on the needs of our communities and those we teach. But the teacher of the church has the ministry of "building up the daily thought and life of the local community of Christians by expounding points of belief and conduct."[19] We devise and engage our strategies for the sake of the Gospel which is for the sake of struggling sinners, that is, all of us. In this kingdom of the world, the Gospel is too rare a visitor to our hearts to ignore the strategy for God's kingdom of grace.

18. Q: When we graciously forgive sin, is the left-hand strategy involved? A: Yes. Nothing about the left-hand strategy forgives sin, but our right-hand strategy is always deployed in the context of the left-hand kingdom. That context influences (is involved in) the timing, location, and consequences of our applying grace to the sinner or sinful situation. For example, I may extend grace to a sinful parishioner or student and be severely criticized for doing so by others. Because I understand the left-hand context, I am not surprised or dismayed by that consequence, and, for the sake of the sinner, I consider my timing and location. Jesus seems to have these concerns in mind in Matt 18:15–20 but applies them in different ways (cf. Mark 2:1–12).

19. *A Theological Word Book of the Bible*, edited by A. Richardson (New York: Macmillan, 1950) 148.

5

The Ministry of Every Christian

Part I—A Needed Perspective

W. Theophil Janzow

Dr. Janzow has served as a pastor, professor, college president, and seminary president. Through these stations and offices he has been a blessing to countless church workers for several decades. This chapter explains the relationship of the teaching and pastoral ministry to the priesthood of all believers.

WHY WOULD teachers of the church emphasize the ministry of every Christian at this particular time in the history of the church? The answer is in the fact that the world's population is exploding and the forces of evil are keeping pace with this growth, thus challenging the church to maximize the use of every possible resource that God has provided to bring the saving message of the Gospel to this post-modern age, and emphasizing that the Lord, through His Holy Spirit, uses not only the church's leadership but the entire Christian community to build and edify His kingdom.

Some of my brethren in the pastoral ministry have told me that they consider it wrong to use the word ministry to describe what Christians do and should do in their daily lives. I have considered this objection and have found it wanting. It is true that some Christians have confused the general ministry of all Christians with the special ministry of the called and ordained pastor of the congregation. Admittedly, this is wrong. But it does not invalidate the biblical fact that all Christians have a ministry, properly understood.

In its use of the word *diakonos* the Holy Scriptures indicate that there are two levels of ministry, the general ministry of every Christian (ministry in the wider sense) and the specific ministry of church workers called by God through fellow Christians (ministry in the narrower sense). Just as the word sanctification has a wider and narrower usage (Luther's Small Catechism, questions 163 and 169),[1] so also the term ministry.

In his book, *Church and Ministry*, Klug spells this out clearly in a chapter titled, "What is the Ministry?" He states:

> The term ministry has both a wide and a narrow sense. In the first sense it refers to the rights and duties which in connection with the Gospel belong by Christ's ordering to the totality of the spiritual priesthood of believers (1 Pet 2:9; Matt 18:17; John 20:23; 1 Cor 3:21ff). Every Christian, young or old, man, woman, or child, shares in this ministry as a believing, baptized child of God. By faith he is a member of Christ's church and His royal priesthood, possessing all the privileges and responsibilities that accompany that station. But ministry in the New Testament also has a more restricted, yet proper and pointed sense, that refers to the office of the public pastoral ministry.[2]

In other words, it is important to emphasize the common ministry of both pastors and laymen and at the same time to clearly distinguish between the two. Note how Klug makes this point.

> "We have this ministry," writes the Apostle Paul to the Corinthian congregation (2 Cor 4:1). He is speaking, first of all, of his office as Apostle, chosen of the Lord, but he is enlisting the people's support in the conduct of the ministry in their midst. God has entrusted the means of grace, Word and Sacrament, to all believers, who as the Apostle Peter affirms, are the royal priesthood (1 Pet 2:5, 9). Christ's mandate (Matt 28:19 and Mark 16:15) makes each Christian a witness for the Gospel to the world around him. . . . However, these are not two ministries, as the above may suggest. Christ establishes only a single ministry for the building of His church through the Word. The mandate which places all believers under the responsibility to make disciples for the Lord is the ground upon which the public pastoral office rests.[3]

---

1. Luther's Small Catechism (St. Louis: Concordia Publishing House, 1986) 146–47.

2. Eugene Klug, *Church and Ministry* (St. Louis: Concordia Publishing House, 1993) 135.

3. Ibid.

Priesthood of All Believers

A primary need in any discussion of the ministry of every Christian is to recognize its relation to the biblical doctrine of the priesthood of all believers. Note how Klug intertwines the two. The term ministry, he writes, "refers to the rights and duties which in connection with the Gospel belong by Christ's ordering to the totality of the spiritual priesthood of believers."[4]

Other Bible scholars have made the same connection. Samuel Nafzger, in an essay delivered at a pastoral conference, cited the writings of early church fathers as equating priesthood of believers and lay ministry.

> Writings from the second and third centuries bear abundant testimony to the importance of the doctrine of the royal priesthood of all believers in the early church. . . . *The ministry of the laity* [my italics] manifested itself in the liturgy, in the recognition and/or election of clerics, in teaching (e.g., Martyr, Origen), in Christian service, in the giving of personal witness to the Christian faith in daily life.[5]

Another scholar, L. W. Spitz, writing in *The Abiding Word*, finds that the relation between the New Testament priesthood of believers and lay ministry was already prophesied by Isaiah who wrote: "But you shall be named the priests of the Lord, men shall call you the ministers of God" (Isa 61:6). Following up on that he finds the ministry of believers as royal priests commanded in passages like Matt 28:19 and 20, Mark 16:15, and 1 Pet 2:9. Spitz concludes: "Because of these powers and privileges given to the New Testament believers, the Prophet exclaims: "O Zion, that bringest good tidings, get thee up into the high mountains . . . say unto the cities of Judah, 'Behold your God.'"[6]

Did Luther find a close connection between the doctrine of the priesthood of all believers, which he championed, and the ministry of every Christian? The following quote answers that question:

> After we have become Christians through this Priest (Christ) and His priestly office incorporated in him by Baptism through faith, then each one, according to his calling and position, obtains the

4. Ibid.

5. Samuel Nafzger, "The Called and Ordained Servant of the Lord and the Priesthood of All Believers." A paper delivered at the Nebraska District Pastoral Conference (Feb. 8, 1999) 7.

6. L. W. Spitz, "The Universal Priesthood of Believers," *The Abiding Word*, Vol. I (St. Louis: Concordia Publishing House, 1946) 328–32.

right and power of teaching and confessing before others this Word which we have obtained from him. Even though not everybody has the public office and calling, every Christian has the right and duty to teach, instruct, admonish, comfort, and rebuke his neighbor with the Word of God at every opportunity and whenever necessary."[7]

Clearly, the ministry of every Christian and the priesthood of all believers are inseparably linked in scriptural doctrine and in the church's understanding and practice over the centuries which need continued and renewed emphasis in this post-modern age.

Abuses

Abuses on both sides of the ministry equation receive a lot of attention these days. Pastors complain that laity want to usurp their God-given prerogatives. Laymen complain that their pastors see them primarily as people who should "pray, pay, and obey," and that their potentials for service in the kingdom are ignored, or, even worse, discouraged. I must focus briefly on this issue.

Raymond Hartwig addresses this problem under the title, *Current Conditions Impacting the Relationship Between the Priesthood of All Believers and the Pastoral Office*. Pastoral abuses are described as follows:

> We collectively cringe to hear of statements made by some pastors today, which fail to regard rightly the priesthood of the believers they serve. These pastors suggest that the efficacy of the Sacrament is emptied in the hands of a lay person, and imply or even maintain that there is no biblical or confessional foundation for the Priesthood of all Believers. They propose that it is an error to assert that in Matt 28:19–20 Christ is commissioning all believers to preach the Gospel and administer the Sacraments. They contend that their fathers and mothers can only offer their own personal forgiveness to their children since forgiveness from Christ can only come from the pastor.[8]

Lay abuses are identified by the same author. He says: "We also cringe to hear and observe the overages committed by some laymen who reduce the pastoral office to something different from its institution by Christ."[9]

7. *Luther's Works*, American Edition, 13:333.

8. Raymond Hartwig, "Contemporary Issues Regarding the Universal Priesthood," in *Church and Ministry* (St. Louis: Concordia Publishing House, 1998) 194–95.

9. Ibid., 195.

As an example he cites the tendency for some lay leaders to judge the performance of their pastor on his CEO-type skills and to approach his pastoral viability according to a "hire and fire" mentality.

Quite obviously, abuses like these should not be tolerated, and every effort must be made to preserve the biblical models of ministry on both sides of the ministry equation.

Is It Just Semantics?

The biblical mandate for both public ministry (narrow sense) and lay ministry (wide sense) is sometimes clouded by misperceptions that tend to minimize rather than maximize Christian outreach. In my youth (many decades ago) people's definition of church work was pretty much limited to the work that pastors do. Laymen, as stated earlier, were expected to "pray, pay, and obey." Someone will say, "That's not the way it was in my congregation." Of course, there were exceptions. But that laymen in general were not challenged to maximize their ministries is a historical reality. It took programs like "Each One Reach One" in the 1940s and "Preaching, Teaching, Reaching" in the 1950s to begin to open our churches to the possibilities inherent in a greater emphasis on the ministry of every Christian.

Did laymen themselves sometimes take the lead in breaking the "pray, pay and obey" perceptive mold? Fortunately, yes! The Lutheran Laymen's League (Lutheran Hour Ministries) and the Lutheran Women's Missionary League (Lutheran Women in Mission) are dramatic examples of laity who "insisted" on practicing their prerogatives of Christian Ministry and outreach. Moreover, virtually every congregation can cite examples of individual members who exemplified the role that Luther had spelled out for laymen, namely, "to teach, instruct, admonish, comfort, and rebuke at every opportunity and whenever necessary."[10]

Many laity today claim that they have never been taught that they have a ministry in their daily lives. Why is this? One explanation is that pastors and teachers have used other words, like service, vocation, or duty to emphasize the role that all Christians are asked to play in maximizing Christ's ministry mandate to the church.

An excellent article in *The Lutheran Witness* titled "Called to our Work," uses the words vocation and calling to discuss the ministry of every Christian. "The fast food worker, the inventor, the clerical assistant, the scientist, the accountant, the musician . . . are all high callings, used by

10. *Luther's Works*, American Edition, 13:333.

God to bless and *serve* (synonym for "minister to") His people and His creation."[11] This shows, it is argued, that this is merely a semantic problem.

But is this all there is to it? My experience suggests that writing this off as a mere semantic problem oversimplifies the matter. In recent years there are growing reports of lay confusion about their roles in ministry and outreach. Individual laymen or small groups of laymen approach synodical leaders (district presidents, circuit counselors, reconcilers) for guidance on how to react to their pastor's "pouring cold water" on their desires to "speak the Word" to neighbors or other unchurched acquaintances. A lay Christian in one congregation reported that he was told, "Don't talk doctrine to your unchurched neighbor; just refer him to the pastor." A former district president suggests that lay complaints such as these are not isolated cases. He reports that some pastors today go so far as to maintain that "there is no biblical or confessional foundation for the priesthood of all believers."[12] This, it must be admitted, is much more than a semantic problem.

Maximizing the Church's Ministry Potential

The church is God's creation. The church is the body of Christ. Christ is its head. The church exists to glorify God, to serve God as living sacrifices, to build up and strengthen believers in their faith, to grow in the knowledge of God's Word, to baptize, to absolve repentant sinners, to celebrate the Supper and, above all, to tell the whole world that Jesus is the Savior.

Everyone needs to be involved in the work of the church. Every aspect of it is essential and crucial to communicate God's promises in Jesus Christ, to tell people both inside and outside the church that "the wages of sin is death but the gift of God is eternal life in Christ Jesus the Lord" (Rom 6:23). All Christians, as ambassadors of Christ, are privileged and obligated to carry out the ministry of reconciliation (2 Cor 5:18–21).

The challenge within the church is a great one. The challenge of mission and outreach to the unbelieving world is, in some respects, even greater. Every resource at the church's disposal must be mobilized as we try to accomplish the ministry and mission mandate of our Lord. Gifted, dedicated, faithful, and outreach-minded pastors are essential. Just as important is the harnessing of the God-given talents of the entire laity. The Apostle Paul surely had this in mind when he told the believers at Ephesus

---

11. Gene Edward Veith, "Called to Our Work," in *The Lutheran Witness* (Oct., 2001) 12.
12. Hartwig, 194.

that God gives the church pastors and teachers "for the equipping of the saints for the work of ministry" (Eph 4:11,12).

The Current Urgency

The ministry of all believers has been essential to the survival, growth, and spiritual edification of the New Testament church from the day when our Lord poured out His Holy Spirit on His disciples on the Day of Pentecost. And the urgency has never diminished. If anything, it is greater in this post-modern world than ever before.

Consider how enormous is the church's evangelism challenge in the world of the twenty-first century after Christ. Not that it ever was easy. But today both the size and the complexity have expanded to seemingly overwhelming proportions.

The world today has a population of more than six billion people. Thankfully, nearly two billion people carry on their foreheads the name of Jesus the Christ. But this means that there are approximately four billion people whom the Apostle describes as "having no hope and without God in the world" (Eph 2:12). Must we not muster the time, energy, and treasure of every single Christian, pastors and people, to heed Christ's pre-Ascension command to be His witnesses, not only in Jerusalem, Judaea, and Samaria, but "unto the uttermost part of the earth" (Acts 1:8)?

Post-modern forces and trends that call for maximum deployment of every Christian in the church's ministry and evangelism challenge are exacerbated by the fact that the world is in a period of enormous change. One social analyst points to a window of opportunity that opened as we turned the corner into a new millennium.

> The bond we share today with the people of past millennial eras is the sense of living in a time of enormous change. . . . When people are buffeted about by change, the need for spiritual belief intensifies.[13]

We must recognize that non-Christian forces are not hesitant to exploit this window of opportunity for anti-Christian purposes. In recent years the number of Buddhists in the United States has grown to around five million, the number of Hindu temples has grown to more than 500, and the number of Moslems exceeds four million. Such encroachments from outside our national borders are accompanied by new religious

---

13. John Naisbitt and Patricia Aburdene, *Megatrends 2000* (New York: William Morrow and Company, 1990) 271–72.

movements coming from inside, for example, the New Age movement. It is estimated that as early as 1987 the number of New Age channelers in the Los Angeles area alone was over one thousand.[14] In addition, there are more than 30 million people in the United States (14 percent) who claim no religious affiliation whatsoever, often referred to as "the unchurched." More than half of the states of the United States have at least 40 percent of people unchurched.[15]

Clearly, the need for involving every Christian in ministering to a world steeped in unbelief and following after a growing array of false gods can hardly be overstated. As the Apostle Peter indicated, every member of the royal priesthood must be invited, urged, helped and trained to be active in "showing forth the praises of Him who has called them out of darkness into His marvelous light" (1 Pet 2:9).

Needed: A Strong Sense of Ministry

The burden of this chapter is to suggest that a renewed and increased sense of ministry (in its wider sense) on the part of every Christian believer can make an important difference in the church's life and activity as it intensifies and broadens its witness impact on a country and a world which is drawn increasingly to follow the false gods of the post-modern age.

We hold that the inspired Word of God, with its message of redemptive love in Christ for all mankind is "the power of God unto salvation to everyone who believes" (Rom 1:16). We also hold that God does not send this message immediately, like a thunder bolt from the sky. He has entrusted the responsibility of proclaiming this saving message to His believing children here on earth, to church workers in the performance of their public ministry, and to all Christians in their private lives. When the Apostle Paul urged the Roman Christians to "confess with your mouth the Lord Jesus" (Rom 10:9), he was extolling the same ministerial role to which Luther referred when he said: "Every Christian has the right and duty to teach, instruct, admonish, comfort, and rebuke his neighbor with the Word of God at every opportunity and whenever necessary."[16]

Ours is a highly competitive society. False god religions promote their ungodly beliefs with the same zeal and fervor as do companies who are hawking their commercial products. It behooves the Christian church not to be timid or half-hearted in its proclamation of the saving truth

14. Ibid., 276–84.

15. Andrew Simcak, "What is Your MQ?" in *The Lutheran Witness* (Nov., 2001) 16.

16. *Luther's Works*, American Edition, 13:333.

(Rom 1:16). "I am the Truth," Jesus said (John 14:6). We must use every resource God has given to its maximum potential to proclaim this Truth both here at home and around the world. It is the only way to salvation for the souls of all mankind.

We have in the past seen some brilliant flashes of strong lay ministry that followed the model of the early post-Ascension church. One example happened in 1930 when a number of dedicated laymen organized the effort that resulted in "The Lutheran Hour" with the dynamic Walter Maier as its first speaker. Other examples could be cited. My prayer is that the same strong sense of dedicated ministry will come to characterize the lives and activities of all believers in the church. As one church leader has challenged,

> We must find better ways of facilitating the priesthood of all believers, one of the church's greatest unclaimed treasures. Our people have the intelligence, the education, the financial resources, the dedication, the love for the Lord and for His church necessary to move this church forward in unprecedented fashion. The development, mobilization and utilization of the people of this church must receive high priority.[17]

Who can doubt that the strong ministries of teachers, directors of Christian education, and pastors as they teach and proclaim the Word with power in their offices, together with the maximum support, participation, and leadership of a dedicated laity in their vocations and callings can, under God, once again turn the world upside down for Christ in a recurrence of what happened in the church's earlier history, another time of enormous change? God grant it, for Jesus' sake!

17. Gerald Kieschnicks, Lutheran Church—Missouri Synod Convention Proceedings (July 14–20, 2001) 114.

6

The Ministry of Every Christian
Part II—Theological Perspectives

RICHARD CARTER

Dr. Carter has served as a director of Christian education, professor, and missionary. His ministry of preparing church workers includes teaching in the U.S., Africa, Europe, and Asia. This chapter reviews the biblical words and concepts for the church's ministry of all Christians including those in church work.

"THE MINISTRY of every Christian"—how much ink has been spilled already on the topic of ministry? How much of the ink involves egos bleeding and life choices threatened? Martin Luther argued that people respond to the Law in two ways: in pride and in despair.[1] Discussions of ministry seem frequently to yield the same responses, if not also anger which may camouflage them. Ministry is God's work, moving people through Law beyond anger, pride, and despair, to Gospel. The intent of this chapter is to assist in that movement.

"ministry, Ministry, and the Office of the Ministry"

Three terms begin this discussion of the ministry of every Christian: ministry, Ministry and the Office of the Ministry. The first term, *ministry*, is a common noun. It refers to helping others, providing energy, empathy, and faithfulness. For example, a nurse ministers to a patient. Introducing a pastor as "This is our minister" implies this basic helpfulness. Helping is the ministry of every Christian.

---

1. "The Smalcald Articles," III, Article II, *The Book of Concord*, translated by Theodore Tappert (Philadelphia: Fortress Press, 1959).

In this article, *Ministry* is also a proper noun. It refers to the particular help given when sins are forgiven. This public duty of pastors may be undertaken by every Christian in personal ways. Luther teaches both the forgiveness we speak to one another and the forgiveness God speaks.[2] Ministry appears in more forms than "forgiveness." The New Testament has no small vocabulary for this Ministry that includes redemption, reconciliation, joy, and light. This is the Ministry of every Christian.

To clarify, giving a listening ear or responding attentively when someone hurts is ministry. The conversation is Ministry when there is accountability before God and forgiveness from God.

The third term, the Office of the Ministry, confesses that God did not leave forgiveness-speaking to the happenstance of human life. "To obtain such faith, God instituted the office of the ministry."[3] Offices such as doctor and president illustrate the Office of the Ministry. The doctor's argument with family members or the president's golf handicap is not a factor in their work; in their office such people should serve us. So also in the Office of the Ministry.

For this Office of the Ministry, some are selected and set aside. The method is analogous to that of a person being selected and set aside to become a doctor. Any pride of place, however, is inappropriate. There may be human, institutional ranking, but there is no ranking of the value of persons. So also not being in the Office of the Ministry is no grounds for discouragement or discounting one's self. The "Office of Medicine" is important, but parents still need to provide day-to-day care of their children.

The three terms are visible in activities, but represent more than activity. The Office of the Ministry is not simply preaching, but the Gospel working in preaching. Serving food is ministry, but food served angrily will not appear as ministry. Ministry expresses a caring relationship.

Scripture demonstrates all three terms. One sees the Office of the Ministry when St. Paul describes his work. Common ministry appears when women care for Jesus and the Twelve. Ministry is demonstrated by Christmas shepherds making known what they had seen and heard. We can see these terms in life as well. A-je, a woman in Hong Kong, Ministers 18 months after she first heard the name of Jesus, distributing Bibles and tracts. The called and commissioned people through whom she came to faith demonstrate the Office of the Ministry. Nurses demonstrate ministry,

2. "The Large Catechism," V:10–13, *The Book of Concord*.
3. "The Augsburg Confession," V, Article I (see German text), *The Book of Concord*.

as do parents, professors, garbage collectors, presidents, day care providers, and the like.

Concentric circles illustrate the relationships among ministry, Ministry and the Office of the Ministry. Label the center circle ministry: the heart of everything is serving God and others. Ministry, forgiving sins, is a particular expression of that central service. The Office of the Ministry is the outer circle God sets in place to serve the other two. Others would see the circles reversed: the center ring of God's provision of the Office of the Ministry energizes the second ring, Ministry, as Christians deliver God's Good News to the world. The largest, inclusive ring is ministry. Every act in all the circles is helpful service. No act stands alone; as priests are part of a priesthood, serving together, ministerial and Ministerial acts are closely linked.

New Testament Words

Commonly in the Greek New Testament behind the English word *ministry* lies the word *diakonia*. *Diakonia* is similar to deacon and deaconess, but "waiter," "waitress," or "server" reflects its meaning. The range of meanings of *diakonia* in the New Testament springs from its basic meaning seen in Acts 6, as "one who waits on tables." This concrete use comes to include a wider, general sense, "to provide or care for . . . . The term thus comes to have the full sense of active Christian love for the neighbor and as such it is a mark of true discipleship."[4] The *diakonia* family of terms includes the specific meaning of deacon in some passages, but the roots of the term imply service. When one considers the Office of the Ministry, or Ministry, or ministry, serving is central.

That ministry means service is more than a matter of definition. The Spirit's use of the common Greek term *diakonia* carries an important implication. "In Greek eyes, serving is not very dignified. Ruling and not serving is proper to a man. . . . For the Greek in his freedom and wisdom there can certainly be no question of existing to serve others." Contrary to Greek assumptions, "Jesus is not merely bringing about a radical change in the academic estimation of human existence and action; He is instituting in fact a new pattern of human relationships."[5]

The reference to Jesus occurs last intentionally in this discussion of servant words. The Word made flesh defines ministry. The ministry of

4. *Theological Dictionary of the New Testament*, edited by Gerhard Kittel (Grand Rapids: Eerdmans, 1964) II:84–87.

5. Ibid.

every Christian is part of the new pattern worked in all human systems by the divine service in the death and resurrection of Jesus. As Luther explains, we "serve Him in everlasting righteousness, innocence, and blessedness, even as He is risen from the dead, lives and reigns to all eternity."[6]

Vocation

In *Ordinary Saints* Robert Benne discusses the "new pattern of human relationships" as it appears in every facet of life.[7] He summarizes daily life in four categories: marriage and family, work, public life, and church. In each category he notes that *all* people have places of responsibility, with *Christians* responding to God's call. In each category, for all people and for Christians, he uses the word *service*. In the Lutheran tradition this is the doctrine of vocation.

Vocation is bigger than a job or a church "job." Vocation is Gospeled people serving at home, in community and in congregation. Christians live under God's command to make disciples but also do God's work in caring for His world. Common daily ministry reflects God's mission. Speaking English slowly with an immigrant or empowering employees to serve customers may set the stage for later Ministry; such ministry is valuable now by engaging in God's creative work.

Vocation demonstrates the unity of physical and spiritual realities that began at creation. There is a temptation to devalue the physical in the presence of the spiritual; the Incarnation and the sacraments counter that perspective. Both Scripture and the Confessions teach, very carefully, that after justification in grace Christians cooperate with God in this physical realm. Some implications of this teaching include:

- Appropriate witnessing at work is valuable, but so is work; both are commanded by God
- "church workers" are also sisters, parents, and citizens
- both performance review and affirmation of Ministry apply to church vocations

In vocation the eyes of faith see God at work, but this is not a romantic view of life. Bosses can be mean, and parenting is sometimes very hard. The choice to remove life support or change the form of church services

---

6. "The Small Catechism," II:4, *The Book of Concord*.

7. Benne, Robert. *Ordinary Saints* (Philadelphia: Fortress Press, 1988).

can be painful.[8] Vocation begins in the cross and baptism because we cannot be saved by our right choices or our own suffering.

This teaching that God calls to common service may be misunderstood. All Ministry and the Office of the Ministry must be ministry. That is inherent in their common term, *diakonia*. However, not all vocation, not all ministry, is Ministry. The casserole is good, but does not forgive sins. Shoveling snow is service but is not itself grace in Christ.

This distinction is too easily and wrongly perceived as diminishing all service other than the Office of the Ministry. Rather the distinction defends the other ministries. If there is no forgiveness, the value of every common task is in doubt. If there is no distinction, one stands fearful in Luther's monastic shoes, asking: "Have my deeds, religious or common, been enough and good enough?" Under the pressure of such questions, ministry collapses. Eternal, egotistical self-defense masquerades behind service to the other. But for the grace of God, no deed nor doer of the deed could stand before God. In the freedom of forgiveness every deed may be a free gift to God and neighbor. We aim to do our best not in order to get to grace, but *within* the grace already given.

Difficulties

The usual translation of Luther's Small Catechism question reads, "What does this mean?" One difficulty encountered in discussing ministry is our ability to be mean with our meanings. We discount and demean ourselves or others by the way we choose to use our words. Our human inventions, the particular ways we choose to follow Scriptural teachings about Ministry, are not themselves divine commands to lord it over others.[9]

Another difficulty in discussing ministry is not having enough meaning in the word. For example, ministry may be thought of as "being nice." Being nice to people in a way that does not confront evils, such as the abuse of drugs or alcohol, is no ministry, no service, except to ourselves. Confrontational ministry is not easy, but necessary.

Discussing ministry and vocation may be difficult also because dying is involved. Physical death may be part of service, whether helping a family at the loss of a loved one or serving at 9/11 Ground Zero and in war. Also, our spiritually dead condition is revealed in service, which may be a reason that pride and despair appear in discussions of this topic. A pastor illustrated this spiritual death when talking about his grumbling while

8. *Issues in Christian Education* (Fall 2001) deals with a number of these issues.
9. "Formula of Concord," Part I: Epitome, X:3, *The Book of Concord.*

shoveling snow for an unidentified grouchy neighbor. Did his story have a lovely ending, such as the neighbor stopped being grouchy or the pastor came to like the nasty neighbor? No. He just did it. In our daily tasks we discipline our Old Eve or Adam by simply doing what must be done, fear or pride or anger notwithstanding. As a woman at church said, "I don't visit the grumpy shut-in because she's nice; I go because I'm supposed to." This vocational reality is part of the baptismal life, the daily dying to our sinfulness.

Lack of Sabbath rest is a difficulty in our service. We are easily hooked, wanting to be good in every time and place, perhaps better than God. There are times when each of us must stretch, do more, work harder. Is it service always to do so? God took a Sabbath after creating; Sabbath is His gift to us in our service.

The underlying difficulty in ministry is sin. Every ministerial act is touched by original sin. God preaches every Christian sermon, but the pastor's desire for power and control, or desire to get by with little effort, is sin. We seldom admit it, but original sin raises its head in the actual sins of all of us in common daily life. "Which sins should we confess? Here consider your station in life, whether you are father, mother, son, daughter, master, mistress or servant." (Luther was gender and status inclusive on the subject of sin!)[10]

To name sin is to move toward absolution. Forgiveness, not our efforts to serve better, liberates for ministry. We serve in the freedom of the Gospel, even with our old sinful self fully attached. No one changing diapers, shoveling snow, or preaching is free from sin; there is likewise no one not died for.

Gospel

The Gospel is the source of ministry and the focus of this chapter and book. Christ died for writer and reader. The resurrected Lord liberates for daily work. A Lutheran high school choir which made a CD illustrates this point. The choir is not *saved* by its beautiful music; not all of the choir's notes are beautiful. What is beautiful, like the beautiful feet described in Isaiah 52, is the choir's word. Texts are clear; the Word gets out. "Jesus, thy blood and righteousness, my beauty are, my glorious dress." While we remain sinners, God saves us wholly in Jesus.[11] The Gospel is not God

---

10. "The Small Catechism," V:19–20, *The Book of Concord*.
11. "The Smalcald Articles," III, article XIII, *The Book of Concord*.

serving so that we try harder to be good; the Gospel is God declaring us good so that we may serve.

Discussing ministry includes recognizing that the Gospel proclaims a cosmic reality, not just a man who loves me. That God gave his only Son is nutshell Gospel, but not the whole story. The resurrected Christ is seated at God's right hand, far above all rule and authority, power and dominion (Eph 1:21). "Through him all things were made; without him nothing was made that has been made" (John 1:3). In the resurrection Christ returned to exaltation, to his universal rule. Thus every Christian service is not simply love to a neighbor, but an exercise of Christ's dominion. Changing a child's diaper is love, to be sure, but joy and victory as well.

The reference to diapers directs us again to the cross. Can diaper changing really be a victory? Can shoveling the neighbor's snow be ministry? Can a pastor's spontaneous comments in a crisis be God serving? God's work in a carpenter's son and God's use of the world's foolishness to save, mean that God can use us to serve. Common service is the mask of God's work, as surely as the cross both hides and reveals God's grace. While we die in service, mortifying our silly, sinful, prideful flesh by common tasks, God works graciously.

Some Reflections

1. The Priesthood of all Believers: What does "the priesthood of all believers" teach about the ministry of every Christian? Misunderstood, it evokes pride: we're better than they are because we don't have priests, or "I don't need someone else to go to God for me." Correctly, 1 Pet 2:9 uses words from Exodus to teach that Christians are a royal priesthood, which is a gift, not an achievement, as Hebrews shows. Further, priesthood and ministry are a shared responsibility. One serves on behalf of others, not one's self. No priest stands alone, but always with other priests, always for other people, always in Christ the High Priest. By Baptism we are made the people of God and holy priests for others.

2. Spiritual Gifts: One mistake of monastic life was its valuing of religious activity above other activities. Some spiritual gifts discussions make the same mistake. Service "within the church becomes regarded as intrinsically more valuable than work within the world, that is within our vocations. After all (so the thinking goes) within the church we are serving the Lord! . . . [T]hose who faithfully labor as witness-bearing Christians in their vocations

are ignored and overlooked."[12] Vocation teaches the unity of the spiritual and physical. All good gifts and calls are God's. "The First Article [of the Creed] provides the foundation and framework for the other two articles. It provides the context and the setting for Christians to serve their neighbors within everyday life and occupations."[13] The Third Article's focus on the Holy Spirit proclaims the Second Article's heralding of the Son who sets people free for the First Article's emphasis on godly service in church and in creation, using natural gifts for divine purposes.

3. Worship and Work: "Divine Service" has become a popular Lutheran description for worship. It applies to daily life as well. In weekly worship God serves, providing sacrament and servers the unique Ministry of the Gospel. At the same time, any service in all of creation is divine. While the sacrament offers the sure promise of grace, no part of creation excludes God working. As Luther states, "Although much that is good comes to us from [women and] men, we receive it all from God through his command and ordinance. Our parents and all authorities (in short all people placed in the position of neighbors) have received the command to do us all kinds of good. So we receive our blessings not from them, but from God through them."[14] God serves in worship and work, in all vocation.

Given the priority of Christ and grace, we may see also a unity of "human service" in vocation and worship. In both we respond to God. In worship we are engaged in the Word and praise which will sustain our daily life. In daily life, along with "rocks, hills and plains," we "repeat the sounding joy," living out God's wisdom and praise.

What kinds of services, activities, or rituals might the church develop to acknowledge and celebrate vocation? Although we confirm and commemorate the faithful who died in the previous year, what ceremonies or rituals might we develop for the living? For those who have started new jobs in the last year? For celebrating God's good work in office, garage and gymnasium as well as harvest?

While we commonly marry and bury, for what other life events or experiences can the church serve its people with ceremony or ritual? Which

12. "Spiritual Gifts: A Report of the Commission on Theology and Church Relations," (St. Louis: The Lutheran Church—Missouri Synod, 1995) 46.

13. Ibid., 47.

14. "The Large Catechism," Part I:26, *The Book of Concord.*

lesser festivals of the church year can help us honor art, teaching and the renewal of society? An understanding of vocation, of ministry, of worship and work, underscores the need to make connections between Word and world for all engaged in ministry.

Conclusion

On the Third Sunday in Advent the Church prays, "Grant that we may know this salvation and serve you . . . through Jesus Christ, our Lord." There is no place for pride or despair when salvation is given freely and all are called to serve in Christ. *Ministry* is a many-faceted jewel. No facet stands alone; all together serve. There are edges to the jewel, and wrongly used it may cut. The jewel is precious, however, and every facet shows the jewel's beauty. So it is with the ministry of every Christian, revealing a precious Gospel for all the world.

7

The Ministry of Teachers

Part I—A New Testament Perspective

KENNETH HEINITZ

Dr. Heinitz, retired as a member of the theology department at
Concordia University (River Forest, Ill.) has taught generations
of Christians, including many church workers. He is the author
of several articles on the church's ministry. This chapter provides
a Christocentric summary of the teaching ministry.

THE MINISTRY of teaching is commensurate informally with the history of God with His people from the beginning. Already in the Garden God instructed Adam and Eve how to live in their created, wholesome relationship with Him.

After the Fall the teaching in part became condemnation, but it was followed and surrounded by Promise. The twofold Word of judgment and promise has constituted the heart of all God's teaching formally and informally through the ages. The Good News of redemption over-against judgment marks the essence of Christian teaching and designates the substance and spirit of Christ's commissioning the disciples to baptize and to teach all nations. It is also the taught song of the church in worship and witness which will culminate in that worship of praise and thanksgiving about the throne at the Second Coming of the Lamb, High Priest, and Teacher.

What does the New Testament say about teaching, about the teacher? Responding to such questions, one needs to distinguish between 1) the Scriptures, and 2) other writings. Subsequent ecclesiastical developments and practices need to be kept distinct, so that one does not read later designated responsibilities and job descriptions back into Scripture. It is too easy to be caught up with concerns about position, status, or office. Scriptural perspectives and priorities must be maintained.

Old Testament Background

It is well to note, in passing at least, the Old Testament background to ministry in the New Testament.

In the Old Testament the spokespersons for God were the prophets and the priests. The prophets were the primary spokespersons. They proclaimed God's Word and instructed the people accordingly. Moses, the historic type of the prophet Jesus Christ who was to come (Deut 18:15; Acts 3:22), was followed by prophets equally noted—Samuel, Elijah, and others. Multi-talented spokespersons and leaders of Israel, their word and work ministerially and prophetically foreshadowed that of the forerunner John the Baptist, of whom Jesus said that none is greater (Matt 11:11). The prophetic activity of the Old Testament prophets including that of John culminated, however, in that of the Son of God, through whom the Father has spoken to us in these last days (Heb 1:2).

Just as the Holy Spirit spoke by the prophets in the Old Testament, so also in the New Testament the Holy Spirit teaches all things and brings to remembrance all that Jesus Christ, The Prophet, has said (John 14:26) and done for mankind's salvation. Having gifted God's people in a variety of ways for the common good (1 Cor 12:4–7), the same Spirit now speaks through all the members of the Body and has given some to be apostles, prophets, teachers . . . (1 Cor 12:28).

Also spokesmen for God in the Old Testament, the priests were given a place primarily in the cultus—the rituals of worship according to the ceremonial law. Along with the prophets, the priests were responsible for the welfare of the people. Some of Yahweh's harshest judgments were pronounced on the prophets and priests for their faithlessness and negligence of the people under their care (for example, Jer 23; Ezek 13; Mal 1 and 2).

Whereas the priests in the Old Testament had a dominant position, the role and function of priests culminated in the person and ministry of Jesus Christ. Although "priest" as an ecclesiastical term has designated a role in many segments of Christendom, the formal priesthood was an Old Testament, not a New Testament, concept. In the New Testament, Jesus Christ is the One Priest. He is both the Lamb and the Eternal High Priest, the Mediator, who has ascended into heaven (Heb 8:1–2). Believers in

Him, His Body—the Church—are the priesthood (1 Pet 2:9) as promised (Exod 19:6).[1]

Jesus' Ministry

Jesus was called and acknowledged as Rabbi, Teacher, Master. He who was and is Prophet, Priest, King, and teacher proclaimed and modeled the "ministry," i.e., servanthood. It is that which He carried out for our salvation, and which He proclaimed and taught.

As given in the four Gospels it was as Teacher, Master (*didaskalos*), Rabbi that Jesus was more commonly known and addressed—together with "Lord," a title of respect as well as a confession of faith in Him.

Jesus Christ was not only called Teacher, which He acknowledged (John 13:13), but He also obviously taught. At the beginning of the Sermon on the Mount, we read that Jesus "opened his mouth and taught them, saying . . ." (Matt 5:2). Just prior to that, Matthew summed up Jesus' early ministry by writing that He "went about all Galilee, teaching (*didasko*) in their synagogues and preaching (*kerusso*) the Gospel of the kingdom and healing every disease and every infirmity among the people" (4:23).

In the four Gospels the words "teach" and "teacher" are commonly used. As expected, the concept of teacher and teaching characterizes Jesus' ministry. We find a good example of this in the Gospel of John. The sequence of Jesus' references to His own teaching and that of His disciples in the future provides insight and structure to the ministry of the Word as a whole.

As recorded in John's Gospel, Jesus emphasized that He came to do the work and will of the Father (chapter 5), and that He spoke as the Father taught Him (8:28). Later, before the high priest's false accusations, Jesus responded that He had always spoken openly, and that He had always "taught in synagogues and in the temple" (18:20). Earlier, when Jesus was speaking to the disciples before He went to the Garden to be betrayed, He promised the Holy Spirit who would "teach" them all things and bring to their remembrance all that He had said to them (14:26).

---

1. Word studies for this chapter are drawn from two standard references: Kurt Aland (ed.), *Vollstandige Konkordanz Zum Grieschen Neuen Testament*, 2 vols. (Berlin: Walter De Gruyter, 1983); and Gerhard Kittel and Gerhard Friendrich (eds.), *Theological Dictionary of the New Testament*, 10 vols., translated by Geoffrey Bromiley (Grand Rapids: Eerdmans, 1968).

This emphasis on teaching the Word, centered in the redeeming work of the Word Incarnate, was carried through to the disciples and the church in general. After His resurrection, Jesus exhorted Peter to "Feed my lambs . . . tend my sheep" (John 21:15–16)—a mission to include teaching, no doubt. That commission had its counterpart in Matthew when Jesus sent the disciples to baptize and to teach all nations (Matt 28:19–20). And when they would be brought before rulers and authorities, they were not to be anxious about their response. The Holy Spirit would "teach" them in that very hour what they ought to say (Luke 12:11–12).

There is no exclusive pattern in the language and imagery of Jesus, however. With reference to the verbs, Jesus characteristically said, "I say," "I tell you," and "I have spoken" (for example, John 16). As Mark, for instance, described the beginning of Jesus' ministry, Jesus "healed" people and "expelled" demons (1:34). He went "preaching" (*kerusso*) throughout Galilee (1:39). Appointing twelve, Jesus "sent" (*apostello*) them out to proclaim/preach (*kerusso*; 3:14). And Jesus Himself, as Mark recorded, taught (*didasko*) the people (4:1), taught in parables (4:2), and taught the disciples (8:31).

As one reviews the verbs that Jesus used both in the synoptic Gospels and in John, there is no one pattern that dominates—although "teaching" stands out as much as any other. The characteristic verbs recorded in the four Gospels in general—like those of Jesus' speaking—are those of ordinary discourse: say, speak, answer, do. In regard to ministry, one could single out "teach," "proclaim/preach," "serve," (*diakoneo*). One might add "sent" and "witness." "Bring or announce good news" (*euaggelizo*) stands out by virtue of the vocable itself, but it is not tied to any one type of position or servant. Position and status are just not part of Jesus' commissioning, exhorting, or sending. Servanthood is: "it is enough" that a teacher and servant be like his master (Matt 10:25).

Also, one observes that there is no apparent distinction in the verbs in regard to authenticity, primacy, or importance. The three more dominant verbs that characterize Jesus' ministry and discourse are "bring good news" (*euaggelizo*), "proclaim" (*kerusso*, often translated "preach"), and "teach" (*didasko*). In Matt 11:1, for example, we read that after Jesus had finished instructing the disciples He went on from there to "teach" and to "proclaim" in their cities. Following that, in His response to the question of John the Baptist's disciples, Jesus spoke of the poor having "the good news preached to them" (*euaggelizo*; 11:5). But of those three verbs—"bring good news," "proclaim/preach," and "teach"—not one appears to carry more weight or authority than the others.

It is interesting to note that in his Gospel John did not use *kerusso* (proclaim/preach; *Konkordanz*, I, 1:691). Neither Mark nor John used the verb *euaggelizo* (bring or announce good news), although Mark employed the noun eight times. Luke used the verb *euaggelizo* ten times, and Matthew only once (*Ibid.,* 462–463). The word "teach" was commonly used in all four Gospels, however, to describe Jesus' ministry and to record His sayings (*Ibid.,* 244–245).

The nouns "overseer" (or bishop) and "elder" with reference to the disciples and others who had been sent came later with the disciples' own ministry as recorded in Acts and the Epistles.

Over-all, as recorded in the Gospels, as Jesus taught and sent the disciples, His emphasis was not on status, office, or position, but on proclaiming the kingdom of God, healing the sick, and casting out demons. The emphasis is on believing, life, servanthood, and the follow-through of faith in Him.

Acts of the Apostles

The book of Acts uses a variety of vocables, but their usage is generally in keeping with what we have found in the Gospels. There is no set or dominant pattern. In his opening remarks to Theophilus, Luke referred to his first account, i.e., his Gospel, about all that Jesus "began to do and to teach" until He ascended (1:1–2).

As Luke began to record the history of the disciples after Jesus' Ascension, he wrote that before casting lots to select a successor to Judas the disciples prayed the Lord to direct them in choosing another to take part in this ministry (*diakonia*) and apostleship (*apostole*; 1:24–25). Later, after the revelation of the Holy Spirit, we read that these early Christians continued steadfastly in the "apostles' teaching and fellowship," the breaking of bread and in prayers (2:42).

In Acts 4 we read that the priests and others were annoyed because Peter and John continued "teaching" the people and "proclaiming" (*kataggello*) "in Jesus the resurrection of the dead" (v. 2). Warned not to speak in Jesus' name they replied that they could not but speak (*laleo*) what they had seen and heard (v. 20). In Chapter 5 we read that after the apostles had been arrested, the angel who released them said that they should go to the temple to speak "to the people all the words of this Life" (v. 20). Luke recorded that when they heard this they "entered the temple at daybreak and taught" (v. 21). Luke wrote further that the disciples, continuing to teach, were reported and forbidden (vs. 25 and 28, respectively), and in a type of summary statement recorded that they did not cease teaching and preaching Jesus as "the Christ" (v. 42).

This varied, yet ordinary, vocabulary characterizes the book of Acts in general. After the stoning of Stephen and the persecution which followed, we read that those who were scattered went about announcing or preaching the Word (8:4). After his conversion, Paul proclaimed that Jesus was the Son of God (9:20). To Cornelius, Peter explained that the Lord had charged them to proclaim Him and to testify fully that He was the One "designated of God to be the judge of the living and the dead" (10:42). In Acts 11, Luke recorded that some of the scattered "spoke" the Word only to Jews, but that others spoke to the Gentiles "preaching the Lord Jesus" (vs. 19–20). Speaking to the people at Antioch of Pisidia, Paul referred to the "witnesses" of Christ's resurrection (13:31). It was this good news that Paul "announced" to them (13:32). After the Jerusalem Council, following their report to the congregation at Antioch, we read that Judas and Silas "exhorted" the brethren with many words and strengthened them (15:32). Luke recorded that Paul and Barnabas remained there, "teaching and preaching the word of the Lord" (15:35). In Acts 20, Paul said to the elders at Ephesus that he had declared (*annaggello*), taught (*didasko*; v. 20), testified (*diamarturomai*; v. 21), and proclaimed (*kerusso*; v. 25) the kingdom.

In keeping with the varied vocabulary, especially the verbs, which Luke used in Acts (as well as in his Gospel), it is interesting to note the four verbs used to describe Philip's ministry—one of the seven chosen to "serve tables" (6:2) and called evangelist (21:8). We read that going to a city in Samaria Philip proclaimed (*kerusso*) Christ to them (8:5). The multitudes gave heed to what he said (*lego*; v. 6). To these people in Samaria as well as to the Ethiopian eunuch, Philip announced the good news (*euaggelizo*; 8:12, 35, respectively). Philip also baptized (8:12, 38).

In Acts, just as in the four Gospels, Luke focused attention on the Gospel of Christ itself. The emphasis is on speaking, proclaiming, declaring, teaching, and announcing the Good News. In the four Gospels, as well as in Acts, it appears that the proclamation itself and the verbs receive more emphasis and are more important than the speakers and the title or position of any one speaker, whether apostle, evangelist, "prophets and teachers" (13:1). In Acts, as in the four Gospels, no one verb has primacy over another, and no one verb designates position or office, and especially no one position or title over another.

Alongside this observation it is interesting to note that Luke and Paul used the noun "apostle" more than did Matthew, John (each once), and Mark (twice). This is distinct from the verb *apostello* (send), which was commonly used by Matthew (22 times), Mark (21 times), Luke (26 times), and John (28 times), although Paul used the verb only four times. One can speculate that Luke, not having been an eyewitness (Luke 1:2), perhaps in deference to the "twelve" and to Paul, used the noun "apostle" more frequently (seven times in the Gospel, 30 times in Acts; *Konkordanz*, I, 1:85–86).

Paul used the noun "apostle" regularly in the salutation of his letters. Throughout his correspondence, he referred to himself in various ways, however, for example, servant (Titus 1:1), ambassador (Eph 6:20), fellow-worker (1 Cor 3:9), steward (1 Cor 4:1). Writing to Timothy in his first epistle, Paul referred to himself as herald/preacher (*kerux*), apostle, teacher (2:7).

But neither Luke nor Paul was hierarchically minded. It is evident that Paul, chief of sinners (1 Tim 1:15), persecutor and the least of the apostles (1 Cor 15:9), was still quite conscious of his apostleship. The two characteristic "uses" of the term other than in his salutations were to assert the authenticity of his teaching which he received from the Lord (for example, Gal 2:6–9) and to defend his ministry against false apostles (for example, 2 Cor 11:12–13).

With respect to the nouns it is almost a cliché to state that "elders" (*presbuteroi*) and "overseers" or bishops (*episkopoi*) are used interchangeably in Acts 20:17 and 28 respectively. We read in Acts 14 that on their first missionary journey Paul and Barnabas returned from Derbe to Lystra, Iconium, and Antioch, and "appointed elders" (plural) in every church (v. 23). In both Acts 14 and 20, whether the elders were older men, leaders of the synagogue as in the Jewish tradition (cf. Acts 15:2, 4, 6), or formally designated servants is not particularly clear. No doubt a transition was taking place.

In his letter to Titus, Paul instructed him to appoint "elders" (plural) in every town (1:5), and then proceeded to describe the qualifications of a bishop (1:7–9). Following that, Paul directly addressed Titus and wrote: "But as for you, teach what befits sound doctrine" (2:1). It is interesting to note that in his epistles Paul used the term "elder" with reference to the public ministry only three times (1 Tim 5:17,19 and Titus 1:5; *Konkordanz*, I, 2:1165).

It becomes clear that these terms, qualifications, and responsibilities implicitly interrelate. There are no sharp lines of demarcation. As recorded in Acts 20, Paul stated, and in his own writings implied (Titus 1:5), that elders were to be "overseers" and caretakers (cf. 1 Pet 5:1–2: elders shepherd the flock by oversight). Paul instructed Timothy to do the work of an evangelist (2 Tim 4:5), and also referred to Timothy as a servant with him (Phil 1:1). In his first epistle to Timothy, Paul described qualifications for bishops (3:1–7), deacons (3:8–13), and (in effect) elders who labor in preaching and teaching (5:17). The responsibilities and qualifications overlap, and in substance are practically identical. In a sense Paul summed up the matter in his second epistle to Timothy when he wrote: "You then, my son, be strong in the grace that is in Christ Jesus, and what you have heard from me before many witnesses entrust to faithful men who will be able to teach others also" (2:1–2).

A Ministry Together

It is evident that these appellations are not definitively set and that the terms as well as the qualifications and responsibilities overlap. It is also evident that "office" is not a category, nor a concern as such. One can not single out any one responsibility or person or title and assign to it exclusively the office of the public ministry. In this respect, for example, neither Stephen nor Philip was limited by the description of his work as described in Acts 6:1–3. Whereas the disciples asked that faithful people be selected to provide attention to the economically needy so that they could devote themselves fully to the ministry of the Word, we read that Stephen and Philip proceeded to proclaim the Word of God and to perform signs. There is no record of either the disciples or the assembly being upset about this. In fact, hearing about Philip's work in Samaria, Peter and John in effect confirmed his proclaiming the Gospel and baptizing by laying their hands on those who had believed and were baptized (Acts 8:14–17).

Prior to that, Stephen "full of grace and power did great wonders and signs" (6:8). His opponents "could not withstand the wisdom and the Spirit with which he spoke" (6:10). Philip, as stated before, proclaimed the Gospel (8:5, 12, 35, 40), performed signs (8:6), and baptized (8:12, 38).

Even with respect to the responsibility given to overseers and elders (including deacons, cf. 1 Tim 3:8–13), in no instance is it exclusive. We must also keep in mind that we are here speaking about nomenclature following Jesus' Ascension. He did not use these terms as such. Somewhat unexpectedly we find that, as recorded in Acts and in his epistles, Paul did not refer to himself as an elder, and Peter did only once (1 Pet. 5:1; *Konkordanz*, I, 2:1164–65). In regard to responsibility one might well remember that James, by writing that not many should become teachers, implied an unlimited scope of responsibility when he further wrote that "we" (including himself) shall "receive greater judgment" (3:1).

The term "prophet" continued in the New Testament but evidently gradually ceased to be used—perhaps ironically in view of the term "priest" which came into increasingly common usage in the second century and following. With reference to John the Baptist, Jesus said that "all the prophets and the law prophesied until John" (Matt 11:13). This implies that both have served their purpose, for Jesus proceeded to say, "And if you are willing to accept it, he is Elijah who is to come. He who has ears to hear, let him hear" (vs. 14–15).

In Acts, for instance, people continued to be called prophets (13:1). In 1 Corinthians Paul wrote that, in contrast to the ecstatic speaker, the one who prophesies "speaks to men for their upbuilding and encouragement and consolation . . . [and] edifies the church" (14:3–4), i.e., one who explains, teaches, and proclaims the Word. Generally, it can be said that "by and large the New Testament understands by the prophets the biblical proclaimer of the divine, inspired message" (*Kittel*, VI:828).

To Conclude

As evident throughout the New Testament, there were teachers. Teachers and teaching are a constant in the Gospels, Acts, and the epistles. There were teachers along with apostles, prophets, workers of miracles, healers, etc.—enumerated rather than ranked in view of the previous context of the harmonious parts of one body (1 Cor 12:14–29). There were also evangelists, bishops, deacons, deaconesses, and elders. The term "teacher" overlapped with other terms, such as prophet, proclaimer/preacher, apostle, bishop, and vice versa. Teaching was a responsibility held in common. Yet, it was a term distinct in itself. Also, "teaching" was a term used to refer to the Word of God in general that was proclaimed and handed on for the salvation and edification of mankind (2 Tim 3:16).

In the New Testament one does not find any particular concentration on "office" itself, such as the high priesthood of Aaron in the Old Testament. In the New Testament any such designation, appellation, or nomenclature was not an issue or an end in itself but always part of the larger matter of proclaiming the Gospel to all nations, to baptize (Matt 28:19–20). Paul's point about himself, Cephas, and Apollos in 1 Corinthians, for instance, dealt with the factions at Corinth, the singleness of the Gospel, and the unity of faith in Christ, not with the office *per se*.

As expressed in the Gospels, Jesus' concern was the proclamation of the kingdom and servanthood. In several instances, the emphasis on servanthood was made in contrast to the disciples' discussion about who would be the greatest (Mark 9:33–36) and to the request of the sons of Zebedee (Mark 10:35–45).

The whole spirit, thrust, and perspective of the New Testament in general is the worship of God, servanthood, the community firm in its trust in Christ, and the fruitful use of the Spirit's gifts to proclaim forgiveness and peace, to baptize, to teach the word, to cast out demons, to heal the sick, to visit those in prison, and to provide food and clothing to the needy.

To that end, teachers together with proclaimers/preachers, deacons, bishops, elders, and evangelists are to teach and proclaim the Gospel and lead the way, so that the ministry of the Church is carried out. Indeed, there is a formal, public ministry of the church as distinct from the priesthood of all believers, but according to the New Testament within that one public ministry there are various ministries.

8

The Ministry of Teachers
Part II—Lutheran Perspectives

JAMES H. PRAGMAN

Dr. Pragman has served as pastor, professor, presenter, administrator, and church executive. He is particularly noted for his preaching and his many years of preparing church workers. Pastor Pragman's writings include the book, *Traditions of Ministry: A History of the Doctrine of the Ministry in Lutheran Theology*. This chapter examines the place of the teacher in the public ministry of the church.

L ET US begin by looking at some variations on that Lutheran question, "What does this mean?" for the teaching ministry:

How do the Lutheran Confessions view teaching and the teaching office? What was Luther's view of the ministry of teachers? How have the traditions of the Lutheran Church interpreted the call to the teaching ministry of the church? How do these traditions view the ministry of teachers and public ministry? Do these traditions see the office of the pastor as the only office of public ministry in the church? How do contemporary statements of The Lutheran Church–Missouri Synod view the office and ministry of teachers? What do Lutheran perspectives disclose concerning the questions and issues about the teaching ministry?

I perceive from these questions some "thought-starters," and these suggest that the old issue is the continuing issue: do teachers have the right—either human or divine—to consider themselves part of the public ministry of the church in a sense similar to the way in which pastors think of themselves as (a part of) the church's public ministry?

Yet I must confess that I do not see why or how further discussions of this issue will do much good. I say that because I think most folks in the church have already fixed in their own minds what the "proper" and "correct" answer must be. Those who are anxious to affirm the ministry of pastors as *the* public ministry of the church do not wish to affirm, also, the ministry of teachers as *the* public ministry of the church. Those who understand the ministry of teachers as the public ministry of the Gospel in the church are disturbed to discover that other "ministers" denigrate their dedication and service by suggesting that they are "ancillary" or "auxiliary." "Ancillary," according to my dictionary, is "subservient" or "subordinate." "Auxiliary," which my dictionary lists as a synonym for "ancillary," is defined in the same terms: "subsidiary," "accessory," and "subservient." People who have devoted themselves to a ministry of teaching in and for the church do not like to think of themselves merely as "ancillary" or "auxiliary."

Scripture and the Lutheran Confessions

But let us not get ahead of ourselves. We should deal more or less directly, at least, with some of the questions implicit and explicit in other chapters of this book. First of all, how do the Lutheran Confessions which were written in the sixteenth century view "teaching" and the "teaching" office?

When our Lutheran fathers in the faith composed the Lutheran Confessions in the sixteenth century, there was no such thing as a Lutheran school teacher as we know that twenty-first century office and ministry. When the Lutheran Confessors commented about "teachers," they were referring to the work of the public ministry, i.e., those who preached the Word and administered the sacraments as parish pastors and priests.

Does that historic truism, however, eliminate the issue? Of course not! An approach to the understanding of the office of the public ministry which draws a straight line, as it were, from one era in history to another without regard for the reality of the passage of time and the developing needs of the church as they manifest themselves over time is neither legitimate nor realistic. God is not going to ask us at Judgment Day if we stood where Luther stood: God is going to ask us if we stood where He wanted us to stand in our age. As St. Paul remarked, "whatever was written in former days was written for our instruction . . ." (Rom 15:4). Thus, we study the Lutheran Confessions and the Tradition/traditions of our theology so that we might learn and be instructed, but our calling is to take that knowledge and apply it to opportunities for ministry which the Lord of the Church is giving the Church in the present age.[1]

1. For further discussion of the Lutheran Confessions see *Called to Believe, Teach, and Confess: An Introduction to Doctrinal Theology*, edited by Steven P. Mueller, Appendix, "The

What I seem to be hearing these days—at least, from some quarters—is that there is *only one office* of the ministry and that *one office* is co-terminous with the office of the pastor. Moreover, the conclusion is reached that this singular arrangement is Biblical and Confessional. Other "ministers" are merely "ancillary" and "auxiliary," i.e., dispensable. Perhaps this summary is a "straw man," but—be that as it may—this summary is the perception of more than a few who function in the church as "teaching ministers" in Lutheran Day Schools. Is that perception and the reality it seeks to reflect valid as a correct assessment of the ministry of a Lutheran school teacher?

At the risk of running roughshod over the feelings of others, let me express the tension this way: is the Church's public ministry "monolithic" or "multifaceted"? Is there more to the office of the ministry than the office of the pastor? And if we want to say that there are ministers other than pastors, does that mean that the office of the pastor is being diminished and belittled? My reading of the Holy Scripture teaches me that the office of the public ministry in the church in the first century consisted of apostles, prophets, evangelists, healers, helpers, widows, pastoring teachers, and others. In other words, St. Paul's letters reveal a multifaceted public ministry. To insist that all of those "offices" or "functions" in the twenty-first century have now of necessity, i.e., by divine decree, been absorbed into the singular office of the pastor is an assumption which requires proof.

"Office" Versus "Function"

We are skirting the issue of "office" vs. "function" in our understanding of the public ministry. This issue, in my judgment, can easily force us into a corner where we find ourselves constrained to make choices between and among false alternatives (cf. St. Paul's response to false alternatives in 1 Cor 3:18–23). It is folly to pit "office" against "function" when discussing the public ministry of the Church: what is the "office" of the public ministry without the "functions" of the public ministry? Some in the tradition of Lutheran theology have attempted to separate office from function, but those who participated in the development of the theological tradition of The Lutheran Church–Missouri Synod[2] recognized that office

Lutheran Confessions" (Eugene, Ore.: Wipf & Stock Publishers, 2005). Many other treatments are available such as *A New Look at the Lutheran Confessions 1529–1537* by Holsten Fagerberg (St. Louis: Concordia Publishing House, 1972).

2. Cf. the writings of C. F. W. Walther on church and ministry. Walther's views are summarized in my book, *Traditions of Ministry: A History of the Doctrine of The Ministry in Lutheran Theology* (St. Louis: Concordia Publishing House, 1983) 140ff. Various biblio-

and function cannot be separated. The office of the public ministry has been established so that the functions of the holy ministry actually happen. If the office of the public ministry does not perform the functions of the public ministry, then, according to the Lutheran Confessions, is there an office any longer?

On the other hand, the functions of the public ministry are also the functions of the spiritual priesthood of all believers. Those functions, according to Luther, are preaching the Word, baptizing, consecrating and administering the Lord's Supper, binding and loosing sin, sacrificing, praying for others, and judging doctrine.[3] But the fact that functions are identical does not mean that public ministry and universal priesthood are identical. A Christian can and must speak the Word of Law and Gospel to others, even though that activity does not mean that such a Christian is now an occupant of the Office of the Church's Public Ministry. The office apart from the functions of the office of the ministry is irrelevant; functions exercised by Christians who do not occupy the office of the public ministry (for example, one Christian admonishing another Christian and speaking the word of forgiveness) do not render the office obsolete and redundant. "Office" and "function" must not be stuck at the two opposing ends of a continuum as though they were in diametrical opposition to each other: they live in mutual relationship with each other and at times in tension with each other but never apart from each other.

What does this have to do with "Lutheran perspectives" on the ministry of the Lutheran school teacher? The church in the present age has inherited an understanding of public ministry which, in practice, has demonstrated itself normally in the work of the parish pastor. The experience of many congregations is that the only "public minister" in the church is their pastor. For other congregations (and, surprisingly, for the majority of those who are listed in the ministerial rosters of The Lutheran Church–Missouri Synod), the ministry consists of pastors, teachers, directors of Christian education, directors of music, social workers, counselors, and other professionals. Congregations which have staffed themselves with a variety of "ministers" have done so because they were led by God's Spirit to share Word and Sacrament through a variety of individuals performing in public various functions of the one office of the public ministry. These arrangements in the actual life of the parish have not led to confusion about ministers and ministries (i.e., who is the "pastor" here? or who is the

graphical sources are identified in notes 53–98 on pp. 201ff.

3. Martin Luther, "Concerning the Ministry" (1523) *Luther's Works* (Philadelphia: Muhlenberg Press, 1958; American edition) XL:21–32. Cf., *Traditions of Ministry*, 15–16.

"teacher" here?)—even though the working out of individual responsibilities and accountability, as well as the question of ministerial authority, can create tension and difficulty in some situations. My own experience, as pastor of a large and multi-staffed congregation, is that teachers do not come forward to occupy the pulpit on Sunday morning, nor do I go into a classroom on Monday morning to teach the daily lessons.

The Church's Various Ministries

When we broach the topic of this chapter, we have to understand the tradition(s) of the past, evaluate them against the Word of Holy Scripture, and then by the light which God the Spirit gives us put into practice the ministry of Word and Sacrament. We do that by receiving with appreciation and joy the various ministries which the Lord has allowed the church to create for the functioning of His ministry in this age, even as we affirm the oneness of the office of the public ministry as that ministry is performed by pastors, teachers, directors of Christian education, and other professionals who *work with* one another as ministers of the Word in the church.

Perhaps as we continue to reflect on the ministry of pastors, teachers, and others called by the Church to minister in God's name, this perspective can help:

> Lutheran theology declares as its central doctrine that the sinner is justified alone by God's grace, for Christ's sake, through faith. To impart the free gift of justification to mankind, the Holy Spirit employs the gospel, using preaching and other forms of proclamation as well as Holy Baptism and the Lord's Supper as instruments of conveyance. Through these means of grace, God reveals and declares to people that He is fully reconciled to all the world, and through those means the Holy Spirit creates, sustains, and strengthens faith in the forgiveness merited by God's Son, Jesus Christ.
>
> Thus, 'all this is from God, who through Christ reconciled us to himself and gave us the ministry of reconciliation' (2 Cor 5:18). This ministry is the determinative goal for the church's message under which the church is to perform all of its functions. It is in the light of its gospel ministry that the church must appraise the validity of all of its activities . . . .[4]

---

4. Frank W. Klos, *Confirmation and First Communion: A Study Book* (Minneapolis, Philadelphia, and St. Louis: Augsburg Publishing House, Board of Publication of the Lutheran Church in America, and Concordia Publishing House, 1968) 192.

9

What's Lutheran about Lutheran Teaching?

Russ Moulds

This chapter sets out several features of the Lutheran tradition
that make its teaching by DCEs, teachers, pastors, and professors
a distinct and lively ministry to and for the whole church.

WHAT DO you mean, you're a Lutheran teacher? Or professor? Or DCE? Christendom covers time and space beyond the dotted lines of the Lutheran tradition, and few of us wish to say that Lutherans have a monopoly on the Christian faith. Yet we maintain that the Lutheran heritage is more than merely a family inheritance or the inertia of our institutions. We remind ourselves that something distinctive characterizes our spiritual tradition, something that yields a great blessing both for Lutherans and for others, Christian and non-Christian, who become acquainted with it.

We can frame this distinctiveness as "distinct from" or as "distinct for." One way to understand (or promote) a tradition is to contrast it with other traditions—such as, in this case, Calvinist Reformed, Roman Catholic, or Wesleyan—and show why this tradition is different. Another way is to highlight how a tradition shares some common features with other traditions and has aspects and additional features that may inform or enhance other traditions.

What exactly is this distinction that makes our efforts as teachers of the church both different and helpful enough to justify our persistence? What do we have to offer that makes the effort worthwhile for all the church catholic? This chapter argues that Lutheranism has much to offer all inquirers, including those who have no coherent tradition at all, but that Lutheran educators must be well versed in their own tradition to make that offering in an engaging and winsome way.

Ten features of Lutheranism give it the contours and landscape of a province in Christendom well worth living in or visiting, a province that contributes much to the Christian commonwealth.[1] The centerpiece of this chapter is a summary of ten key insights about the Gospel that emerged from the Wittenberg Reformation and that constitute our Lutheran heritage. By surveying all of them at once, we can gain a sharpened appreciation of what makes our teaching distinctive and worthwhile and what we have to contribute to the spiritual lives of all who may study with us.

Reasons to Read On

Before conducting that survey, however, we have reasons why this review is important. Given our common fallen predicament, some of these reasons have to do with our falling short of who God calls us to be. This, of course, is in part why teaching is necessary (cf. Jer 31:34). But by and large a survey of our Lutheran distinctions is very positive and inclusive in the large and eternal sense of that word. Here are four reasons for reviewing a list of our Lutheran distinctions.

First, much like the church's first century when Paul sought out Gentiles in each city's marketplace, our world today is a bazaar of spiritualities. Perhaps the most telling example of spiritual diversity and fragmentation is the Oprah Winfrey Show, but spiritual alternatives are now everywhere. People are spiritual beings and now, as always, they are seeking some orientation to the eternal (cf. Eccl 3:11).

But amid the diversity, people find very few orientations that have a coherent tradition of convictions hammered out through years of careful study of the Scriptures, and fewer still that locate their spiritual well being in God's promises rather than in their self-justifying spiritual projects and personal efforts.[2]

---

1. This territory image deserves critique. The role of Lutheranism has been an important debate since the Diet of Augsburg and the Augsburg Confession in 1530. Should we understand Lutheranism as a movement, a denomination, an ecumenical servant of orthodoxy to all church bodies, or in yet some other way?

2. In its richest connotation, tradition is not a wooden, static set of behaviors enacted out of mindless habit, but a set of beliefs, arguments, convictions, and practices thoughtfully worked out as a meaningful worldview by a community over time. When Tevya in "Fiddler on the Roof" sings about "Tradition!" he sings about the denotation of tradition in certain customs in his community rather than the tradition itself. Alasdair MacIntyre (1981, p. 207) has written extensively on tradition as a community's narrative history and identity.

Lutheranism gives us such a tradition. It gives all of us a defined base line from which to start and then explore a spiritual orientation. It gives Christians and non-Christians a worked-out set of convictions about life, God, and the world He loves. It is no small service to provide all interested parties with such a tradition against which they can estimate their own and other (often less coherent) views. What's more, our presentation of our tradition will perforce include the Gospel itself and its power to create faith in Christ and transform lives.

Second, Christianity always has its elements of folk religion. "Plaque Christianity" hangs in homes and classrooms everywhere: "When God closes a door, He opens a window," and "Who I am is God's gift to me; who I become is my gift to God." The point here is not to rant about pious and frequently misleading religious platitudes. These will always be with us. The point is that a fresh, informed, and congenial integration of the Reformation's insights about the Gospel in our teaching can prompt our students beyond any folk religion they may embrace.

Third, and related to folk Christianity, those distinctive Reformation insights of the Gospel help prevent the Christian's slide into excessive pietism and subjectivity. We Christians, and Lutherans in particular, always deal with the tension between the objective truth of God's revelation of himself in history through Jesus Christ, and our own personal, subjective (and important) experience of that truth. This tension was the source of many of the ancient heresies that continue with us in various forms today. A tradition of worked-out and examined convictions about the Gospel helps people both new and seasoned in the faith to avoid construing God's work among us as merely God's work in me.[3]

Fourth, the Lutheran tradition—this set of insights about the Gospel that has given Lutherans their distinctive heritage—serves as a blessing to the whole church by helping to distinguish the Gospel as good news. The devil, the world, and the sinful self are all engaged in spirituality campaigns, but they all conduct them by enlisting us as the captains of our own campaigns. Their hymn is not "Lift High the Cross" but lift high yourself. And institutions of education are notorious for teaching their unsuspecting students the many human merit systems, be they academic, social, or athletic. The Lutheran Reformation developed these insights and applications of the Gospel to our human institutions to make our sharing

---

3. A related problem is reducing faith to rigid, dry dogmatism. A living faith tradition as we are discussing it here offsets such wooden orthodoxy by sustaining dialog across and within the generations of believers, and with inquirers. This Spirited exchange keeps faith active in love.

the Gospel lively and formative, and keep it as God's intervention rather than our spiritual invention.

The Three *Solas*

The three Reformation solas are a good introduction to the Lutheran insights and serve as sure referents for exploring and examining them. Each of the insights described later in the article is an extension of these solas, just as our ministry of Lutheran education is an extension of the insights. Together these provide a helpful way to understand the integrity of our tradition in the Gospel that we share with fellow sinners. That's the purpose of this chapter: to recall what distinguishes this Lutheran heritage as a Christian tradition that genuinely serves the church and the world that God so loves.

Sola Gratia (Latin for grace alone) is the heart of the Reformation. Luther's breakthrough to the Gospel—that is, when the Holy Spirit broke through to him with the Gospel—came through Rom 1:16–17: "For I am not ashamed of the Gospel: it is the power of God for salvation to everyone who has faith, to the Jew first and also to the Gentile. For in it the righteousness of God is revealed through faith for faith, as it is written, 'He who through faith is righteous shall live.'" Luther realized that the required righteousness Paul describes in Romans is not God's righteousness of judging and punishing sinners, nor our active but impossible righteousness of obeying the Law. It is God's active righteousness accomplished in us and on our behalf not through the Law but by a different Word of God that became flesh and dwelt among us, full of grace and truth. Hence, God's active righteousness in Christ becomes our passive righteousness as a gift (*gratia*):

> I realized it was to be understood in this way: the righteousness of God is revealed through the Gospel, namely the so-called "passive" righteousness we receive, through which God justifies us by faith through grace and mercy. . . . Now I felt as if I had been born again. The gates of heaven had opened and I had entered paradise itself. (Oberman, 165)

Among the many implications of grace alone is the assurance that God's Yes (2 Cor 1:18ff) is to all people of all times and all places. While "Lutheranism" may to some sound parochial in the worst sense (and has at times been practiced that way), the Lutheran tradition gives us both a compassion and a set of convictions for sharing, teaching, and dialog that reaches out with God's love to everyone.

One helpful way the Reformers kept faith as a sola rather than a duet of God and man was by emphasizing faith as trust. The phrase they used was *fiducia cordis*, "trust in [or of] the heart." Since it is the nature of promise to create trust, and God alone can make the promises of the Gospel (*sola gratia*), then faith also is God's work alone—and this secures our faith which alone can embrace God's promises. Early on, Luther had thought that faith was a virtue or trait imputed by the Holy Spirit which we then put to work to lay hold of grace, much as we use the virtue of honesty to work rightly with truth. But as his reading of Scripture clarified the Gospel, he understood faith as the Holy Spirit's changing the heart by means of God's Word and creating our very thirst and desire for God's grace.

The second *sola*, then, is *sola fide*—faith alone. While God's gifts of forgiveness, deliverance from death and the devil, and life everlasting are for everyone, this grace, conveyed to us through Word and sacraments, comes only through faith in Christ. This "faith alone," without our effort, contribution, cooperation, reason, or strength, keeps the Gospel as truly good news. It reminds us that our right relationship with God does not rely on anything we do—which as sinners we might do wrongly—but on what God alone does for us. In terms of *sola fide*, what God the Holy Spirit does is create our faith in Christ.

Teaching in the Lutheran tradition, then, is quite distinct from (though not necessarily hostile to) teaching as moral development or character education, which would seek to inculcate the proper virtues of intellect, conscience, and emotion. Valuable as these virtues may be, they are not the basis for education—though they may be related in some ways to the fruit of the Spirit (Gal 5:22) which is the outcome from our training in a righteousness that comes by grace alone.

The third *sola*, Scripture alone (*sola scriptura*), forms a triad with the first two solas. Samuel Nafzger writes, "Luther's insight that salvation comes by grace alone through faith alone cannot be divorced from 'on the basis of Scripture alone.' For it was directly as a result of his commitment to Scripture that Luther came to rediscover justification by grace alone through faith alone."[4] This rediscovery came as Luther pursued his vocation of teaching. Teaching by its nature is concerned with content as well as personhood and always has a *telos* or ultimate aim in mind (Fenstermacher

4. Samuel Nafzger's brief treatment of the Solas is helpful here. That section is posted on line at http://www.lcms.org/nafzger2.HTM, "What Do Lutherans Believe?" This Introduction is also a reminder that these solas and the Gospel insights of the Lutheran Reformation are worked out thoroughly in the Lutheran Confessions as found in the *Book of Concord*.

and Soltis, 1986, p. 8). In the Lutheran tradition, Scripture alone serves as our source and norm for assessing the spiritual nature and direction of our teaching ministry. How directly we relate this source and norm, and our ultimate aim, to curriculum is one of our on-going discussions, and in our tradition it should be. It has been since Wittenberg. However we may address this issue locally and specifically today, the three Reformation solas suggest at least ten implications that relate the Gospel to the Christian life and inform our discussions. Together these create a living tradition that shapes the scope and purpose of our educational ministry in powerful ways at all levels.

Ten Lutheran Distinctions

What follows next is a digest of these ten insights. Other students of the Lutheran tradition may list them and summarize them differently.[5] The point here is to present them, however briefly, so that we can continue to ask and seek to answer, "What's Lutheran about Lutheran teaching, anyway?" (Standard references are noted for each distinction and are cited in the bibliography.)

1. The Spiritual Is in Relation to the Material

Different from the misleading notion that the spiritual and the material are isolated from each other and even hostile to each other, Lutherans recognize God's divine work and blessing in "things visible and invisible" (Nicene Creed). God's work, while mysterious, is nevertheless plain to us in the physical world not only in creation but also through Jesus' incarnation and resurrection, and in the sacraments. When Paul writes in Col 1:16, "For in him all things were created in heaven and on earth, visible and invisible . . . all things were created through him and for him; he is before all things and in him all things hold together," Paul is not endorsing pantheism but is saying all things have their being and reason in God. If a parable is an earthly story with a heavenly meaning, then all of life is a parable with a spiritual meaning implicit in it. As Lutheran educators, we are surrounded by spiritually loaded incidents and events every day. We can

5. These insights are not all exclusively Lutheran, and other theological traditions share many of them. Some prefer to consider these insights as "authentically Lutheran" rather than "distinctly Lutheran." Readers may also note the conspicuous absence of several important themes such as the priesthood of all believers, *ecclesia semper reformanda* (the church is always reforming), and others. Please note such omissions as you talk with others about what is Lutheran about Lutheran teaching, and see other chapters in this book.

help students learn to see the spiritual intersecting with the secular by addressing selected events. We can be especially helpful by teaching others to distinguish folk religion and reverent superstitions (*deisidaimonia*)[6] from ways of divine intervention confirmed by Scripture (Kolb, 1993, p. 16).

2. The Freedom and Bondage of the Will

Christians often speak imprecisely about "free will" as if we all have a will freed from sin and its damage. Lutherans are careful to recognize that the human will apart from the restoring work of the Holy Spirit is tainted by sin and that "The mind that is set on the flesh is hostile to God; it does not submit to God's law, indeed it cannot, and those who are in the flesh cannot please God" (Rom 7:8). A freeing of the will comes only through a trusting relationship with God, empowered by the Holy Spirit. This freeing comes with faith and is completed at our resurrection. Apart from this freedom, we have only a limited will. We can choose a brand of clothing, a marriage partner, or to make a charity donation, but we cannot choose for the goodness and righteousness of God in our lives and actions. Our students of all ages often confuse this real freedom with claims about free choice in a world that is diverse in every way. Our choice of expressions and instruction about the freedom and bondage of the will can help them sort out this confusion (Dillenberger, 1962, p. 166).

3. Two Chief Words: Law and Gospel

Law and Gospel, of course, apply to everything about the Christian life and about sharing our Christian faith and life with others (see Walther, 1986). One important application of the distinction between Law and Gospel is the difference between legalism and antinomianism. Legalism is the belief and use of God's Law as though laws, rules, regulations, and consequences can solve sin, motivate good behavior, and create Christian community. This amounts to an idolatry of the Law. Antinomianism (Latin for "against rules") is the belief that because God has forgiven us and freed us from the curse of the Law's punishment, we no longer need the Law. This amounts to cheap grace. Christians, whatever their age, often seek refuge in these two errors. We can help them avoid these errors by how we express and

6. The Greek word *deisidaimonia*, as found for example in Acts 17:22 and 25:19, can be translated as religion or as superstition. It literally means "fear of the demon-gods" and was used to indicate recognition of God or the gods mingled more with fear than with trust; superstitious though not in a wicked sense; and attributing to God that which is not truly characteristic of God or authentic about His actions.

apply our rules and consequences in the classroom, how we instruct for life together in Christian community, and where we direct them for genuine refuge from all the ways in which the Law and its demand for righteousness threatens us: "I have another righteousness and life above this life which is Christ the Son of God who knows no sin or death but is my righteousness and life eternal, by whom I shall be raised up and delivered from the bondage of the Law and sin" (Luther, *Commentary on Galatians*; Dillenberger, 1962, p. 106).

4. Simul Iustus et Peccator

This Latin translates as "at the same time justified and sinful" and captures one of the great biblical paradoxes that characterize the entire Christian life. The catechism applies it in the ideas of "old Adam" and "new you." As Christians we continue to live with our sinful nature and experience its influence until we die. But we simultaneously live as new creations of God despite this continued sinful condition. So Paul confesses, "I do not do the good I want, but the evil I do not want is what I do" (Rom 7:19), yet declares, "Anyone who is in Christ is a new creation, the old has passed away, behold the new has come" (2 Cor. 5:17). Paul denatures the paradox only in Christ (see Rom 6) and resolves that, despite our sin, "You must consider yourself dead to sin and alive in Christ Jesus" (Rom 6:11). Our students, young and old, often think in only one category or the other. We can help them recognize the simul paradox by responding to their inquiries about our life together with that practical theological question: "Why do you want to know?" In other words, who wants to know about this issue—the old Adam or the new you? We need to articulate and practice community so that the certainty of the Gospel enables sinners to live together in an uncertain world as the saints of God (Dillenberger, 1962, p. 99).

5. Two Kinds of Righteousness

All Christians possess two kinds of righteousness, one that is not their own and one that is. All Christians need help with distinguishing while sustaining both of them (Dillenberger, 1962, p. 159). Lutherans recognize a righteousness that makes our life and relationship with God right, good, and fulfilled. This rightness comes to us as a gift from God and not through any efforts or ideas of our own. Luther called it an alien righteousness coming down from God through Christ in a vertical relationship. We also recognize another righteousness that makes our relationship with other people right, good, and worth living. In this horizontal relationship with others, our rightness consists in loving our neighbors as ourselves through our works and actions. This second righteousness is a kind of "donated" righteousness, as we use the gift of alien righteousness and extend it to others in our words and deeds. The Lutheran tradition educates people to clearly acknowledge, distinguish, and foster both kinds of righteousness—the first through God's Word and promises, the second as fruits of faith in Christ through stirring one another up to love and good works (Heb 10:23–25).

6. *The Hidden God and the Revealed God*

Through the centuries, many observers have noticed that people are incurably religious, having endless ideas about God and what he is like. All cultures and societies have devised forms for both worshipping and denying God or gods they vaguely sense exist or at least wonder about. Lutherans also have noticed that people constantly speculate about "the hidden God." Typically this speculation, based on guesses and inferences from nature, imagines a God who is majestic, glorious—and threatening, i.e., the "hidden God of the Law only," says Luther (see Dillenberger, 1953, p. 101). The God revealed to us through Jesus' life, ministry, death, and resurrection discloses a different picture. In Jesus, we see God in weakness, humility, and mercy. While it is true that in Jesus we catch an occasional glimpse of kingdom, power, and glory, we mainly see "crib, cross, and crypt" in the Gospel accounts (see Kolb, 1993, p. 20). This is "the revealed God" in the God-man, Jesus Christ. Our teaching and practice within a living community of humility, service, and compassion are part of God's project to reveal himself to us in Jesus through external and accessible Word and sacrament, not through our speculation and guess work about what remains hidden (Deut 29:29; Heb 2:8–9).

7. *Theology of the Cross and Theology of Glory*

Rather than seeing God hidden in suffering and crucifixion, many Christians seek God in the majesty of his creation (Rom 1:20), in the power of nature (Ps 8:3), or the glory and terror of his Second Coming and judgment (Rev 6:15). While these are certainly biblical themes, none of them as such can help the sinner damned under the Law and wrath of this mighty, majestic, and glorious God. Therefore, Luther followed Paul in regarding these themes as secondary to all God was doing through the humiliation and death of Jesus: "For I decided to know nothing among you except Jesus Christ and Him crucified" (1 Cor 2:2). Not nature and creation, not miraculous events in history or individual lives, not judgment and the close of the age, not any manifestation of power, but the cross and broken body resurrected—that's the emblem of our theology and our image of God now. Our theology of the cross locates God and glory where for all the world's imaginations there can be nothing divine. As Hebrews puts it, "But we see Jesus, who for a little while was made lower than the angels, crowned with glory and honor because of the suffering of death, so that by the grace of God he might taste death for everyone" (Hebr. 2:9). Our students, like our culture in general, are often looking for God in all the wrong places. We need a coarse, splintered, bloodstained cross in every quad and courtyard to which each of our lessons and policies can be nailed. (See Kolb, 1993, p. 20ff; McGrath, 1985, p. 148.)

8. Christian Liberty

Early in the Reformation, Luther composed a maxim within which he sought to locate all Christian decisions. His couplet has kept thoughtful Christians busy for centuries working out its implications. He began his treatise on "The Freedom of a Christian" (see Dillenberger, 1962, p. 42) this way:

> The Christian is free lord of all, subject to none.
> The Christian is servant of all, subject to all.

Since the Gospel is true that God's grace actually covers all our sin and that nothing can separate us from the love of God in Jesus Christ (Rom 8:39), then the Christian has perfect liberty to choose and act in any way she or he believes is in keeping with God's Word and coming kingdom. Abraham was prepared to slay his own son. With great distress, Ezra ordered the divorce of Jews who had married non-Jews. John the Baptist recklessly engaged in moral criticism of Herod. Luther questioned but quietly sanctioned the bigamy of one of Germany's princes. Bonhoeffer joined in the effort to assassinate Hitler. The Gospel frees us to make difficult decisions because no action or choice, however wise or wrong-headed, can cancel the saving power of the Gospel. Paradoxically, that same Christian is also the most humble servant or *doulos* (Greek for "slave") to every neighbor. That Christian must make choices and take actions that serve others both temporally and eternally. This Christian liberty, then, is the liberty both to take action and to serve. The Christian is empowered and emboldened to enact this servant liberty by the absolute promise of the Gospel that no work of ours can jeopardize what God has already done for us in Christ. Therefore, Luther declares, "Sin boldly—but believe more boldly still." This is not an ethic of rules or simplistic means-and-ends principles. Rather, we need curriculum and policy for education that informs inquirers and equips students with a sound understanding of servanthood, a growing knowledge of God's Word, and a bold trust in His promises.[7]

9. The Two Kingdoms

Since the fall there are, in fact, two kingdoms or realms of God, not just one. This is a linch-pin doctrine of the Reformation. The right-handed kingdom, as Luther called it, is God's kingdom of grace that is ruled by the grace of Christ in which the Holy Spirit by the power of the Gospel makes Christians and forms disciples. The left-handed kingdom is God's secular kingdom of the world that is ruled through law by people in various stations of temporal authority to preserve order in a fallen, sinful creation. God has established both kingdoms. Only the Gospel can prevail in the right-handed kingdom, not the Law. The Law is the primary authority in the left-handed kingdom, sustaining order in a fallen creation so that the Gospel can be proclaimed (cf. Matt 24:14). Christians in their vocations are called to live simultaneously in both kingdoms. This is not easy to do. Lutheran educators must exist and conduct their ministry in both kingdoms. This is not easy to do. The teaching ministry inducts students into this two-kingdom living. This is not easy to do. We have the difficult task of instructing both through curriculum and policy so that all of us learn to rightly distinguish and not confuse the two kingdoms even as we must learn to live effectively for God in both. The two-kingdom doctrine gives us our basis for participation in politics, the sciences, the arts, business, and all other human activities in the left-handed kingdom. Because these are our activities and works in the temporal realm of the world, our participation—right, wrong, or otherwise—cannot alter what God has done for us in his realm of grace apart from our works (see Paul's powerful statement in Rom 8:31–39). Understanding the two realms is Luther's key for us in doing education that preserves the Gospel yet enables us to explore any and all human claims about truth, beauty, and a life well lived. (See Dillenbereger, 1962, p. 363; Braaten, 1983, p. 123.)

---

7. A related theme that deserves attention is *adiaphora*, that area of Christian conduct that is neither commanded nor forbidden by God's Word. For an extended study of this important topic, see Graebner (1953).

10. Vocation

"God gets up every morning and milks the cows." With this peculiar claim, Luther sets out another linch-pin doctrine of the Reformation that complements all the others: the doctrine of vocation (1 Cor 7:17ff). When the farmer milks his cows, he is doing God's work every bit as much as any monk or priest (or Lutheran teacher or pastor). By milking those cows, the farmer provides sustenance for people either to continue their own lives for another day as God's people in service to others or to live another day and have the opportunity to hear the Gospel and come to faith. So Lutherans insist that every Christian has a vocation, or a calling to faith and Christian living, and that no one vocation is more pleasing to God than any other. Lutheran Christians honor God by honoring all people in all stations of life that provide service, work, care, and respect for others. The smallest child learning her ABCs and the oldest retiree providing care for that child have vocations from God. Lutheran education does more than pay occasional lip service to vocation. It designs to help students link the call of the Gospel to productive human activity as ways to share God's goodness, especially his great goodness in Christ. (See Veith, 1999, p. 71.)

Conclusion

Some have suggested that the most effective way to offer Christian education today is to emphasize that our education is Christian and de-emphasize that it is Lutheran. This point has merit in the sense that 1) Lutheran education has at times been exclusive and ethnocentric, and 2) most people are no longer much interested in denominational boundaries. A constructive take on this view is that we highlight the Christ of Christian education and avoid denominational triumphalism. The danger, however, is that we may end up marketing a store-brand Christianity that conveys little substance for shaping a Christian life. This strategy may be ineffectively casuistic and misleading, especially in secondary and higher education.

By contrast, a Lutheran education that deliberately communicates the biblical, Lutheran tradition and ethos will do students a world of good, both for this world and the world to come. Non-Lutherans, believers and unbelievers alike, will receive a distinct, historically extended, community-embodied worldview located in sources they can access and evaluate as grounds for standards, judgments, authority, the good, and meaning and purpose. What's more, these sources and ideas are *sola gratia*, *sola fide*, and *sola scriptura* in nature. In these times of spiritual diversity, no one needs just one more bland, vapid, church-affiliated education. We do others a great disservice by veiling in merely generic education the goodness of God who has revealed Himself in Jesus Christ. Instead, we have a heritage and the resources to present to them an identity and a community they can consider seriously and against which they can compare other claims.

Meanwhile, Lutherans will receive an account and induction into their own community that does not isolate and inoculate them from the world, but prepares them to understand the world and bring to it that Word of life for today and eternity.[8] The Reformation insights into the Gospel are not intended to return us to the sixteenth century any more than the Reformers' study of the early church fathers sought to recreate the world of the Roman Empire. The Gospel is God's message of reconciliation for all people of all times. These insights of the Lutheran tradition give Lutheran education a distinctively Gospel-oriented substance and structure. Being distinctive in this evangelical way is not sectarian provincialism. Rather it makes us a province with open and inviting borders for all who might glimpse, desire, and receive with joy that abundant life in Christ.

---

[8] Much has been written in recent years about the relationship of the church to the modern and post-modern world. See Hauerwas and Willimon (1989) for one effort to consider how the church can remain distinctively in the world but not of the world. Also Menuge (1999) presents an engaging assortment of essays on the church in the world.

10

The Call and the Will of God

Russ Moulds

This chapter clarifies several common issues connected
to every Christian's calling and to the practice of calling
workers to the public ministry.

THE TEACHER of the church addresses a variety of questions from fellow Christians and from non-Christians about God's will. We, ourselves, also ask some questions, especially when we have to deliberate a call to some particular ministry. This chapter addresses some common themes about God's will and prompts inquiry for further discussion. It applies to these themes and inquiry some insights about the Gospel from Luther's book, *The Bondage of the Will*, his *Commentary on Galatians*, his *Treatise on Christian Liberty*, and from the doctrine of vocation.[1]

Case 1: Dan's first serious struggle with the question of God's will came during his first call, yet had nothing to do with his Lutheran school placement. Rather, his confusion came from being jilted in the name of God. He met Nancy, a congregational member, early in his call. They dated and enjoyed each other's company. As the months passed, the compatibility seemed right, and the relationship grew. Beginning to think of marriage, Dan cautiously and sincerely mentioned the idea to Nancy. To his relief, she didn't balk at the possibility. Dan deliberately brought up the topic from time to time, and Nancy seemed steadily receptive—until one spring night when Nancy called and said they had to talk. As the conversation unfolded, Nancy emotionally yet firmly informed Dan that

---

1. Two brief, helpful books that address themes related to the call and God's will are *The Christian's Calling* by Donald Heiges (Philadelphia: Fortress Press, 1958) and *The Spirituality of the Cross* by Gene Edward Veith, Jr. (St. Louis: Concordia Publishing House, 1999).

they could not marry: praying about the matter, Nancy had concluded that it was God's will that she not marry Dan. Stunned yet respectful, Dan did not believe it was his place to challenge God's will. He agreed to break off the relationship. Three years later he was still unmarried and still confused about what had happened.

Case 2: The third article of the Apostles' Creed raises questions about death and funerals. During an eighth grade religion lesson, students shared experiences of deaths in their families, relating how Jesus' death and resurrection sustained their trust in God's care and promises. Rachel raised her hand and, without waiting to be called on, quietly reported that when her grandpa died last year, someone at the funeral approached her and her mom and told them in a sympathetic voice, "It was God's will that your grandpa died." Rachel then asked, "Did God really want my grandpa to die?"

Case 3: Paul did not get the job even though he was qualified and had an excellent internship. The company flew him out to their headquarters for a battery of tests and interviews which he passed "with flying colors." All of his documentation was submitted ahead of schedule. He got great reviews from the company personnel office. Though several entry-level positions were available, he got no offer. When the turn-down phone call came, Paul was devastated since his hiring had looked like a sure thing. The only thought Paul could summon to console himself was that it just wasn't God's will and that God had another position for him somewhere else.

Case 4: Kelly had a call and she didn't know what to do. She was ready to graduate certified for both high school and middle school ministry. The placement office had sent her credentials to a school with an opening in its departmentalized seventh and eighth grades. The congregation's call included the exact parish duties Kelly desired. With the pastor's and principal's support and encouragement, all the circumstances seemed right. The congregation was waiting, the days were passing, but Kelly couldn't give an answer. Was this the place God wanted her to be? Maybe she should wait for a call to a high school. Why didn't God give her a sign or some indication of what she should do?

What Do You Say?

Marriage, death, occupation, professional church work—all important events and decisions that compel the Christian to ponder God's will. What sorts of things do you say about God's will? What would you say to Dan, Rachel, Paul, and Kelly? What do you say as you face your own important life events and decisions? Whether you're a candidate for placement or a veteran church worker, understanding the "God's will" discussion is an essential part of doing our ministry.

Since the people we serve face these issues every day, part of our call as a teaching minister of the Gospel is to speak biblically and helpfully to others about God's will for them. Also, part of our competence in ministry includes applying biblical principles about God's will in our own lives. Few concepts are more vexing and perplexing to Christians, and, for church workers, the subject pertains especially to the call. Consider a few of the many questions the subject provokes:

- Does God have a particular planned outcome for my decisions? Does he have a preference?
- Since God is all-powerful, is it possible for me to violate God's will?
- To what extent does God intervene in human affairs and change the course of events? In what ways does he and does he not intervene?
- Does God have a plan for my life? If so, what sort of plan is it? Is it a life "map" or "program"?
- Has God pre-selected someone for me to marry? Chosen an occupation for me? Called me to work in the church? How would I know? On what basis would I know this?
- How should I deliberate my first or next call in a God-pleasing way?

Fraught with many questions, the concept of God's will is also plagued by many conflicting answers. Christian bookstores display books from various authors, each offering diverse views and solutions to the mysteries and secrets (real and claimed) concerning the will of God. Exchange on the topic of God's will in adult Bible class or a college bull session offers as many answers as participants. These questions also contain important theological and philosophical ideas such as freedom and determinacy, the nature of revelation, and our source and norm for what we teach and what we say. We cannot unpack such large themes here (see suggested resources at the end of the article). However, we can examine some of the confusion over the "God's will" discussion. Also, we can apply a few basic Lutheran insights about the Gospel to this discussion and to our understanding of the call.

An instructive place to start is Deut 29:29: "The secret things belong to the Lord our God, but the things revealed belong to us and to our children forever, that we may observe all the words of this torah." There are, then, secret councils that belong to the Divine Majesty of God to which we do not have access. This insight will keep us modest and humble in our discussion of God's will. We won't presume to penetrate God's secret councils and omnipotent will which are beyond our comprehension. Yet God has revealed some of himself to us in Christ and the Scriptures, and we can locate our discussion of God's will in this revelation.[2]

Back to Law and Gospel

The Lutheran heritage actually says little about God's will in the typical sense of God directing or orchestrating our choices and decisions. Though this lack may not sound helpful at first, such silence is a significant clue to examining our thinking about God's will and our deliberating a call. The *Book of Concord* addresses the subject of will in terms of our sinful will and God's desire or will for our salvation (see the index listings and cross-references under "Will, of God"). The systematic studies of biblical doctrine do not include treatments about God planning events and decisions in our lives. Instead, they simply acknowledge God's constant presence and his general providence for our daily needs without trying to detect any special will. Consonant with the real complexity of life, sin, and faith, Luther's discussions of God's will are correspondingly practical and complex. Luther located our Christian freedom in his teachings about God's calling or vocation.[3] This rich and important concept not withstanding, Luther's statement about 1 Cor 9:19ff begins to set his teaching apart from the usual things we say and hear about God's will. He notes that the Apostle Paul

> ate, drank, and lived with the Jews according to the law, even though it was not necessary for him. With the Gentiles, he ate, drank, and lived without the law, as they did. For only two things are necessary: faith and love. Everything else you are free to do or leave undone. Therefore, you may do everything for the sake of

2. Luther discusses the hidden and secret will of God in *The Bondage of the Will*, tr. J. I. Packer and O. R. Johnson (Grand Rapids, Mich: Fleming H. Revell, 1957). For an introduction to this theme, see Paul Althaus, "The Freedom of the Gracious God," in *The Theology of Martin Luther*, tr. Robert Schultz (Philadelphia: Fortress Press, 1966).

3. See Luther's "The Freedom of a Christian" in John Dillenberger, ed., *Martin Luther: Selections from His Writings* (New York: Anchor Books, 1962). In *Luther on Vocation* (Philadelphia: Muhlenberg Press, 1957), Gustaf Wingren provides a thorough treatment of Luther's ideas about God's will and Christian freedom. See especially "The Concept of Freedom," "Cooperation," and "Stundelein."

one [situation or person], and for the sake of another refrain from everything, and in that way treat all impartially.[4]

Gustaf Wingren's book, *Luther on Vocation*, explains: "Sovereignty of love before the law involves a creative factor whose expression it is impossible to foresee, since it can steadily open up fresh and unsuspected perspectives for life's activity. In this connection we must recall Luther's frequent statements about the freedom of the Christian 'to do and to omit.' Through this freedom, faith and relation to God attain real significance for vocation, and vocation is shaped solely according to the needs of others."[5]

Or as St. Augustine (from whom Luther took his cue) insightfully asserts, "Love God, and do as you please."

What do these assertions mean for us? "Do as you please" does not mean we have a license to sin or indulge the preferences of our own weak flesh—Augustine begins with the First Great Commandment (and also the Second by implication)! Historically, Lutherans have not troubled themselves much about discerning God's will; also, whatever others may be saying about discerning a divine will about this or that decision, the Bible takes God's providence for us as a given. In most Bible stories, efforts to penetrate God's secret designs are discouraged (for example, 1 Sam 28; John 21:20–23). Apart from the Ten Commandments' moral implications about our decisions, the Bible does not address God's preference of this decision over that decision. Even so, this observation today seems counter-intuitive and needs further discussion.

An important slant the Lutheran tradition gives to the subject of God's will is the biblical interpretive principle of Law and Gospel. This principle teaches that all God reveals to us should be understood in terms of Law—what we are to do, not to do, and how we are to be—and Gospel—what God has done and continues to do for us and for our salvation. Now consider that life's events and decisions are areas of our activity: what we do and don't do. To search for God's will or preference for us about behavior in our domain of activity means to look for a Word of Law; that is, a commandment to rule what we are to do. This search drives us back to Scripture and the moral code of the Ten Commandments. Apart from these Commandments expressing God's moral will for our lives and

---

4. Wingren, 95. Note: because his writings are many and varied, Luther scholars caution us to be careful about citing Luther quotations selectively. However, certain themes such as vocation, God's will, and man's will are well established in the Lutheran tradition.

5. Wingren, 147.

conduct, we draw a blank in finding prescriptions for particular personal decisions. (We will consider the Gospel and God's will in a later section.)

"God Has a Plan for Your Life"

Where, then, does so much talk about God's will and our decision making come from? Return to your Christian book store, examine the available books and, for the most part, you will find authors writing from a theological perspective that traces back to John Calvin. Calvin, the brilliant Swiss reformer of the church and younger contemporary of Martin Luther, wrote one of the most important works of the Reformation, *The Institutes of the Christian Religion*. Despite much agreement, one significant point of difference for Luther and Calvin was the doctrine of predestination. Like many other thoughtful Christians, Calvin struggled with the puzzle of why some are saved but others are not. With trepidation, he concluded that people were predestined by God to their eternal state, either heaven or hell (a view that Lutherans label "double predestination"). Since Scripture says nothing about God predestining anyone to hell, Luther and his spiritual kin have consistently denied double predestination, insisting with St. Paul that "God would have all men to be saved and come to a knowledge of the truth" (1 Tim 2:4).[6]

Later Calvinist theologians (notably the Puritans in America) extrapolated double predestination to include a divine "plan" or "will" of all events in people's lives, elaborating this perspective especially from God's attributes of sovereignty and omnipotence. Lutherans, by contrast, did not move to such extra-biblical inferences. Luther acknowledges God's sovereignty and his hand in all that happens but insists that we cannot comprehend this mystery. We can only sometimes detect God's hand after the fact and then only roughly at best. Thus, Lutherans have sustained a more modest position of silence about matters on which God's own Word is silent and have instead focused on the salvation that God has clearly willed for us from the cross. (Cf. 1 Cor 2:2. Also see the *Formula of Concord*, Solid Declaration, XI, "Election.")

Present popular thinking about God's will comes chiefly from one expression in particular, popularized by one of the most widely used tracts of all time, "The Four Spiritual Laws," distributed by Campus Crusade for Christ. The tract begins, "God has a plan for your life." This expres-

---

6. Some theologians and Bible teachers in the Reformed tradition are moving away from this mechanistic view of God's will. See, for example, Gary Freisen, *Decision Making and the Will of God* (Colorado Springs, Colo: Multnomah Press, 2004).

sion has shaped the views of countless Christians on the subject of God's will. Consider for a moment what this expression suggests. What comes to mind for many people is a "cosmic computer" image of God's will. God has keyed into history a plan or program for all the events of our lives, and our lives are the printers that are turning out the results. What this expression provokes for many Christians is an anxious search for a copy of the program or at least a print preview of what is supposed to come next.

The "God has a plan for your life" view also employs a small collection of oft-cited Bible verses such as Jer 29:11 and Prov 16:9. Jeremiah does prophesy God's assurance in saying, "'I know the plans I have for you,' says the Lord, 'plans for welfare and not for evil, to give you a future and a hope.'" The context of the chapter, however, clarifies that God's words are addressed to Judah in Babylon (29:1) and that the plan is to return Judah to their homeland after a period in exile (29:14). This plan is good news for Judah and for us because God's will is to bring forth the Messiah from the family of David in the tribe of Judah. The text is God's Word for us, but it is his Word for us because it is about his salvation for us in Christ, not because it refers to some life script or program. This realization about Jer 29:11 is at first a bit alarming for some who have never checked its context and meaning. However, the text truly comforts us as we further realize we need no longer puzzle over undisclosed divine plans and instead can entrust our welfare and all life's events, good and evil, to God's revealed plan of salvation (see Rom 8:28 and 29–39).

Similarly, Prov 16:9, "A man's mind plans his way, but the Lord directs his steps," is often used to infer some life script or plan as though the verse could be paraphrased: "We may lay our own plans in life, yet the sovereign God will have his way by intervening and re-directing our choices and life events according to his own perfect will." But such a mechanical view of a Hebrew proverb would be quite foreign to a devout Israelite who already knew how God directed his steps: with the Torah, the written books of Moses. The parallelism in the proverb is an antithetical contrast of the heart of sinful man and God's good direction (cf. Ps 1 and Ps 119). This assessment gives us a different sense of the proverb: "We sinful people may plot out our ways and intents on our own, but God gives us better directions for enacting those ways in the words he has given to us through Moses [and we would add Jesus]."

The Popular Expressions

Though we should not be hypercritical about words (1 Tim 6:4), the language we use and don't use about God's will is important because language reflects our beliefs about God. Some of our expressions are harmless pieties ("God bless you" following a sneeze), and some echo biblical content ("See you next year, God willing" recalls James 4:15, "If the Lord wills, we shall live and we shall do this or that"). But our language is often not biblical and can be misleading. Consider these common examples:

- Make sure you're at peace about this decision. (Was Jesus at peace in Gethsemane?)
- Maybe the Lord is trying to tell you something. (How would you know? On what authority would you say so?)
- I hope God shows me his answer to my problem soon. (Does he have a specific answer in mind? How would you know?)
- Are you seeking God's will in this matter? (Does he have a particular preference about your decision?)
- Whenever God closes a door, he opens a window. (This is from Mother Superior in "The Sound of Music"!)
- I feel God is leading me in this direction. (Are our feelings a reliable guide to knowledge about God?)
- Don't worry—God has a plan for your life in this situation. (Is this what Scripture means by "plan"?)

All these expressions reflecting common beliefs about God and his will deserve our attention. Not that all popular views are bad, for some of the examples can, with effort, be aligned with biblical content. But these expressions have a catch: that being right with God is up to us. They imply that God is a map maker, and it is up to us to be wise and holy enough to find and follow the map; or that he is a cryptographer, and it is up to us to be clever enough to decipher his codes. They imply that, beyond the Ten Commandments, we should search for pre-selected decisions or preferences that God has about every detail of our lives (a notion questionably inferred from Matt 10:29–30 where Jesus' concern is not about hairs or feathers but salvation). These expressions neglect that "the secret things belong to God."

Though we tend to use such expressions, the Bible does not. For instance, Paul's carefully crafted language in Acts and his letters never says anything like, "I had an impression that God was telling me to go to Rome, and I felt that he was leading me to seek his will for me there, so maybe God is telling you in Rome to be ready for me." Despite the absence of such language in the Bible, these expressions are present in the everyday life of the church, including our call processes. An application form used in placing church workers on a district call list begins the essay portion with this instruction:

> Specify the type of position and area of ministry in which you feel God is leading you and in which you have a strong desire to serve.

How does one feel the leading of God? The expression could be taken in different ways, but does suggest that we search ourselves for some still, small, but inaudible voice. The first problem with this idea is that Scripture nowhere instructs us to equate our feelings and emotions with God's will. Though we should remain cognizant of our emotional responses as important content in decision making, we have no authority for trusting such impressions as divine. Rather, our internal feelings are transient and often unreliable. Instead, God has given us his external and reliable Word. The second problem with such language is that the expression "still, small voice" comes from the story of Elijah in 1 Kgs 19 where God speaks to Elijah softly but clearly, telling the prophet in an audible voice to get back to Israel. Inner impressions and feelings are not God's will, and we are not to use them to second guess what we don't know God isn't telling us.

A prayer offered in corporate worship on behalf of a candidate considering a call was worded this way:

> Lord, please lead [candidate's name] to make the decision that is pleasing to you.

The article, "the," casts this petition into theological question and the candidate (and us worshipers) into consternation. By saying "the decision" rather than "a decision," the prayer leader signals that the candidate can satisfy God's expectations only by making one specific choice. This signal implies that any choice other than "the" decision will move the candidate out of what some have called "God's perfect will." If she makes the wrong decision, the candidate moves into a fearsome predicament with God by deciding contrary to God's plan (usually called sin). She is now acting and living out of harmony and fellowship with God (more sin). By this reasoning, she not only risks God's wrath but also misses the blessing God had in store for her had she made the right decision. What's more, this was a call to an important position of leadership, and she has probably convoluted God's will for the calling body. But such prayer language and its implications are distant from what Scripture actually says. God gives us his Word in Christ and the Scriptures, and apart from some direct, specific revelation, God does not prescribe our life choices. (Paul's decision in 2 Cor 2:12–13 is a good case study.)[7]

A memo circulated to announce a church worker's consideration of a new vocation and location read:

> [Church worker's name] asks our prayers and counsel as he seeks to discern God's will for his life and ministry and that of his family.

The language concern with this statement is semantic. If seeking to discern God's will for one's life means turning to God's Word for a study of "leading a life worthy of the calling to which we have been called" (Eph 4:1), then well and good. But if it means (as it often does) resorting to inner impressions or other tactics for divining a secret will of God, this language misleads the Christian into unnecessary agonizing and uncertainty.

Many Christians at one time or another do agonize over making a life decision they fear may be outside God's will. They may know God's grace well enough to realize God will not abandon them in that decision or because of it. Yet they are still provoked to search for any hidden divine choice or preference for that specific decision such as deliberating a call. At this point, they may employ two other tactics for detecting this phantom will of God.

Some would have us place a fleece before the Lord, a scheme from Gideon in the Book of Judges. God in a verbal revelation specifically promised Gideon an assured victory over Israel's enemy, Midian (6:11–24). But Gideon began testing God's promise by asking for signs (6:36–40). Gideon asked God to dampen a sheep skin exposed to the night's dew but keep the ground dry around it. God complied. Then Gideon had the temerity to ask God to confirm his promise again by reversing the sign the next night, keeping the fleece dry but the ground wet with dew. Gideon's lack of faith has been wrongly interpreted by some Christians as an endorsement to search for God's will by seeking signs. Though God, in his infinite patience and to preserve Israel, tolerated Gideon's weakness and granted the signs, the context of Judges establishes that such sign-seeking betrays a lack of trust in God (cf. Judg 8:22ff; Matt 12:38ff).

Others would direct us to life's changing circumstances and events as indicators of God's will. This variation of sign-seeking is the "Maybe God is trying to tell you something" approach. A mild parody will illustrate:

---

7. A related theme to explore is the leading of the Holy Spirit. That theme is important but beyond the scope of this book. A place to begin is "The Holy Spirit and the Conversion of the Sinner" and "The Sanctified Life, or New Obedience" in Kolb, *The Christian Faith*.

Lord, I'm looking for a Godly spouse, and I think Susan may be the one. But your will, Lord, your will. So if that's your will, God, have me run into her tonight at the library. Or maybe tomorrow night. Actually, any time in the next month will do, Lord, but the sooner the better. Excuse me now, Lord, but I've got to get to the library. Amen.

The assumption is that since God is aware of all life's circumstances, he must be arranging them to send us messages about his will. The assumption is mistaken in that it attempts to read the secret things of God with a connect-the-dots method. Life's circumstances are entangled with sin from the devil, the world, and the sinful self, and the Scriptures says nothing about reading circumstances for God's will in some oracle-like fashion. The assumption also confuses the doctrine of predestination. Predestination refers to salvation for those elected to faith, not to life events and decision making (see Rom 8:28ff and Eph 1:3ff).

For Freedom Christ Has Set Us Free

Scripture does make important and clear Christocentric statements about God's will. The center and focus of all Scripture is Jesus. Jesus says, "You search the Scriptures because you think that in them you have eternal life, and it is they that bear witness to me" (John 5:39). At the end of Luke's Gospel, Jesus explains that to rightly understand Scripture, we must realize that "everything written about me in the Law of Moses and the prophets and the psalms must be fulfilled" (Luke 24:27, 44). Luke continues:

> Thus it is written that the Christ should suffer and on the third day rise from the dead, and that repentance and forgiveness of sins should be preached in his name to all nations, beginning from Jerusalem. (Luke 24:46–47)

The will of God, as Paul says, is that all people would be saved and come to a knowledge of the truth about Jesus (1 Tim 2:4). That's the plan. That's what the Bible means when it talks about God's plan:

> For he [the Father] has made known to us in all wisdom and insight the mystery of his will according to his purpose which he set forth in Christ as a plan for the fullness of time, to unite all things in him, things in heaven and things on earth. (Eph 1:9–10, RSV)

The word used here for plan is the Greek noun *oikonomia* from which we get the word economy—ordering, managing, or administering a house or property. The word does not connote a plan in the sense of a script or agenda for every event but rather a master plan for managing a larger purpose or goal. In this case, the "house and property" under management are "all things in heaven and earth," and the goal is to unite them all in Christ whose purpose is "that repentance and forgiveness of sins should be preached in his name to all nations." God's will is that the Law work repentance among us sinful people and that the Gospel bring us to forgiveness and a saving faith in Christ. That work being done, we are then empowered by the Spirit to "lead a life worthy of the calling to which you have been called (Eph 4:1)." Such is the life of freedom living under God's grace (Gal 5:1).

The alternative understanding of God's will as trying to decode some unrevealed divine script would mean a life under the Law. This kind of life would mean always trying to live up to expectations that God never spells out. It would mean living in the shadow of "ought," anxiously wondering what God would have us decide in any important situation. It would mean endless attempts to distinguish between those important situations where we believe God has some individual plan for our actions and those trivial matters that we manage ourselves (marriage? a summer job? lunch?). It would mean constant uncertainty about our relationship with God and, thus, uncertainty about our salvation.

By contrast, God's actual will for us is that we live under grace. The Law shows us our sin, drives us to God's promises, and serves as our guide for behavior, but it does not make us "at one" (effect atonement) with God. Christ alone intercedes for us. Thus, through him and with him we are now all daughters and sons of God. This relationship is the reason Luther in his *Treatise on Christian Liberty* insists both that, "A Christian is a perfectly free lord of all, subject to none; and a Christian is a perfectly dutiful servant of all, subject to all."

The Christian is absolutely free, forgiven by God's grace and liberated in decisions and actions from any condemnation of the Law. Yet this freedom is no license for sin and serving the self (Gal 5:13) since the Christian is also totally a servant, submitting all decisions and actions to the work of God's kingdom to serve the needs of others' temporal and eternal well-being. The apparent contradiction of free and slave is not an unsolvable paradox (like sinner/saint). It is harmonized under the purpose of God's kingdom: that all might be saved and come to a knowledge of the truth. The Christian considering a call is free in this decision. We are free to accept the call, and we are free to return the call to the calling body. In either event God's providence continues to work in his quiet and hidden ways through our decisions and activities (Phil 2:12–13). God's grace prevails, and his kingdom still comes for us. Our language, discussions, prayers, and letters of acceptance and decline sometimes obscure this freedom. We can better express ourselves about calls and God's will when we speak in terms of Christian hope, liberty, and responsibility.

11

To the Teacher of the Church: "Follow Me!"

Jane Fryar

Dr. Fryar has served as a Lutheran elementary teacher, college professor and administrator, and editor of instructional materials for the church. She is the author of many articles and books including *Go and Make Disciples*. This chapter provides practical, biblical guidance for considering our calling and our calls.

"FOLLOW YOUR passion!" I heard this advice several times as I struggled with a substantial change in position description proposed by the Lutheran university at which I have been teaching. Having spent two years as an instructor at the undergraduate level, I was now being asked to assume the role of graduate dean—a position requiring far less teaching and far more leadership and administration.

Several people who know me well and who care about me told me, "Follow your passion." And no doubt, most career counselors and the ubiquitous head hunters that populate the Internet would applaud this advice. However, it struck me as a strangely North American way to go about hearing the call of God, an approach reflecting more closely the narcissism of Western thought popular in the late twentieth and early twenty-first centuries than the biblical view of vocation articulated by Luther and refined by Christ's church down through the centuries since. Having emerged from the call process, having made a decision, and having placed the hours of deliberation behind me, the advice to "follow your passion" strikes me as even more odd, more incongruent.

Follow your passion? Yes, perhaps, but what has my passion to do with determining my God-given vocation? What has my passion to do with God's will for my life? And in what directions do I turn as I seek day by day to follow Jesus' call, "Follow me"? These are all key questions as we consider what our Savior-God might have in mind for us, as we ponder the directions in which he might want to channel our service.

Sky Writing?

During *Fair St. Louis*, that wonderful rite of passage from the season of spring into deep summertime, businesses from all over east central Missouri hire small planes to circle the greater metropolitan St. Louis area, especially the crowds that flood the Arch grounds and spill over into riverfront cafes and downtown shops. These planes trail banners behind them with messages akin to the old-fashioned sandwich boards worn by unemployed factory workers during the Great Depression: *"Eat at Joe's!"* *"This is Ford country!"* or *"Russ's Lawn Service!"*

How much simpler the call process would be if our Lord would simply hire a biplane to trail an explicit message tied to our life's vocational direction: Teach in Springfield! Or so we may think. But how much simpler would it be—really? Scripture records several "case studies" in which Yahweh got just that specific with his servants, and yet we see reluctance and resistance more often than not.

Take Moses, for example. Instead of a sky writer, the Creator of the universe conscripted a burning bush through which to deliver an explicit message from heaven. Moses received an "immediate call," to use a term common in our ecclesiology; Yahweh spoke to Moses directly, rather than through an intervening agency like a congregation or Christian school.[1]

Did Yahweh's direct and explicit voice coming from that bush make Moses' decision process easier? We might think so. At least, we may find ourselves assuming that if we were to hear an audible voice, we would respond in instant obedience, packing our bags for Egypt then and there! Yet Scripture records the dialog by which Moses did his best to convince the Almighty to reconsider or even withdraw the call he had so vividly and unmistakably placed on Moses' life. Are we as reluctant as Moses was to believe God's promise to use us in his service? Do we, like Moses, resist God's call? I urge you to read the entire account from Exod 3–4 and then reread the verses excerpted from that text below:

> The LORD said [to Moses], "I have indeed seen the misery of my people in Egypt. I have heard them crying out because of their

---

1. Contrast the immediate call of Moses with the "mediate" call of David to be Israel's future king. This call was delivered in secret by the prophet Samuel who served as an intermediary; Samuel "mediated" Yahweh's call (cf. 1 Sam 16).

slave drivers, and I am concerned about their suffering. . . . So now, go. I am sending you to Pharaoh to bring my people the Israelites out of Egypt."

But Moses said to God, "Who am I, that I should go to Pharaoh and bring the Israelites out of Egypt?"

And God said, "I will be with you. And this will be the sign to you that it is I who have sent you: When you have brought the people out of Egypt, you will worship God on this mountain." Moses said to God, "Suppose I go to the Israelites and say to them, 'The God of your fathers has sent me to you,' and they ask me, 'What is his name?' Then what shall I tell them?"

God said to Moses, "I am who I am. This is what you are to say to the Israelites: 'I AM has sent me to you.' . . .The elders of Israel will listen to you. Then you and the elders are to go to the king of Egypt and say to him, . . . 'Let us take a three-day journey into the desert to offer sacrifices to the LORD our God.'"

Moses answered, "What if they do not believe me or listen to me . . . ?" [At this point, God gives Moses two miraculous signs to perform as proof, then Yahweh says,] "If they do not believe you or pay attention to the first miraculous sign, they may believe the second."

Moses said to the LORD, "O Lord, I have never been eloquent, neither in the past nor since you have spoken to your servant. I am slow of speech and tongue."

The LORD said to him, "Who gave man his mouth? Who makes him deaf or mute? Who gives him sight or makes him blind? Is it not I, the LORD? Now go; I will help you speak and will teach you what to say."

But Moses said, "O Lord, please send someone else to do it."

Then the LORD's anger burned against Moses and he said, "What about your brother, Aaron the Levite? I know he can speak well. He is already on his way to meet you, and his heart will be glad when he sees you." (NIV)

To be honest, this incident comes uncomfortably close to mirroring my own conversations with Jesus at several times over the past three decades of my own service as a teacher in his church. Perhaps as you read the dialog, you, too, heard echoes of your own excuse-making and reluctant obedience to the call of God in your own life. As we consider the incident, several truths about God's call pop off the page. Consider these:

- God did not call Moses for the purpose of exalting Moses. Rather, he called Moses in order to honor the Covenant he had established with Abraham centuries earlier. That Covenant had passed down to Abraham's descendents, the nation of Israel—a nation that had lain enslaved in Egypt for 400 years. The nation had all but forgotten Abraham's God, but he had not forgotten them. Nor had he forgotten his Covenant. Yahweh had seen his people's affliction, heard their cries, and known their sufferings. And in response Yahweh, in essence, said to Moses, "I know, so you go!" Similarly today, our Savior-God calls people into full-time, public service in his church, not to aggrandize us, but because he knows how much the world he so loves needs to hear the message of salvation won on Calvary's cross.

- Moses felt unworthy and inadequate, and indeed he was! At the time 80 years old, Moses had spent the last 40 of those years following flocks of sheep around Sinai's desert. Early in life Moses had been "instructed in all the wisdom of the Egyptians" (Acts 7:22). As Pharaoh's adopted grandson, the teenage Moses had likely been slated for a position of power in Egypt's government one day. But Moses had gone into self-imposed exile at age 40 after he committed cold-blooded murder, killing one of the slave masters in Pharaoh's employ. In the mercy of God, Moses' inadequacies did not disqualify him from service, nor did his sins. And neither do ours! In calling Moses, Yahweh acted in line with his eternal Covenant of grace toward both Moses and his people Israel. In calling us, the Lord always acts toward us and his people in keeping with his Covenant of grace through the cross of his Son.

- God wasted nothing from Moses' past. For the prophet, as for us, "in *all things* God works for the good of those who love him, who have been called according to his purpose" (Rom 8:28; NIV, *emphasis mine*). Moses' childhood experiences in Pharaoh's palaces and his years in Egypt's libraries, schools, and diplomatic circles stood him in good stead as he fulfilled God's call to lead his people. So did the four decades of solitude, meditation, and repentance in the desert following the murder he committed. In similar ways, God redeems the histories of those he calls today.

- The proof of God's call came after Moses had responded in obedience, not before. Note the precise wording of Exod 3:12. Here Yahweh promises, "I will be with you, and this shall be the sign for you, that I have sent you: when you have brought the people out of Egypt, you shall serve God on this mountain." True to his word, God met Moses on Sinai as Israel, now a free people, camped on the plain beneath the mountain (see Exod 34:1–28). First Moses went, then he saw the sign. So too in our lives, the "sign" we may seek comes most often after we have acted in response to the call of God.

Happiness?

God's call on Moses' life, undeniable and immediate in the technical sense, did not result in Moses' instant and glad obedience. Though Moses could not have known all that lay ahead, the triumphs and frustrations, joys and grief, he did know that responding to that call would change his life forever. The comfort of his daily routines, the ease of living in familiar surroundings, the relative safety of home and family, the predictability of "life on the farm"—all of this and more disappeared as Moses left his sheep and his wilderness sanctuary for the Nile delta. The Savior's call often leaves our own lives similarly disrupted and inconvenienced.

This should not surprise us. The various calls God places on the lives of his human creatures all tend to intrude on our personal plans and hopes. Perhaps disturbing to our self-centered, sinful nature, but true nonetheless, the Lord of the universe does not pace across heaven wringing his hands and fretting about how to make us happy. Concern for our happiness—at least in the self-absorbed ways in which our culture defines that term—appears far, far down on God's list of priorities for our lives.

You see, our heavenly Father has a much higher, much fuller destiny in mind for us. He intends no less than our transformation into the image of his Son, our Savior:

> But whatever was to my profit I now consider loss for the sake of Christ. What is more, I consider everything a loss compared to the surpassing greatness of knowing Christ Jesus my Lord, for whose sake I have lost all things.
>
> I consider them rubbish, that I may gain Christ and be found in him, not having a righteousness of my own that comes from the law, but that which is through faith in Christ—the righteousness that comes from God and is by faith.
>
> I want to know Christ and the power of his resurrection and the fellowship of sharing in his sufferings, becoming like him in his death, and so, somehow, to attain to the resurrection from the dead.
>
> Not that I have already obtained all this, or have already been made perfect, but I press on to take hold of that for which Christ Jesus took hold of me.

> Brothers, I do not consider myself yet to have taken hold of it. But one thing I do: Forgetting what is behind and straining toward what is ahead, I press on toward the goal to win the prize for which God has called me heavenward in Christ Jesus.
>
> All of us who are mature should take such a view of things. And if on some point you think differently, that too God will make clear to you. (Phil 3:7–15; NIV)

God's first call on our lives is primary—the call to salvation, to faith in Jesus, crucified and risen, the call to eternal life and to the increasing freedom of full Christ-likeness (2 Cor 3:16–18). The Holy Spirit sealed that call in your Baptism and in mine. Far from being merely a memory from long ago and far away, that water is alive in us, producing powerful and ongoing effects even now. The water is alive and active—in us and through us!

> Jesus stood and said in a loud voice, "If anyone is thirsty, let him come to me and drink. Whoever believes in me, as the Scripture has said, streams of living water will flow from within him." By this he meant the Spirit, whom those who believed in him were later to receive. (John 7:37–39; NIV)

Like an eternal fountain gushing up from an infinite aquifer, the water of life overflows from all of God's people into the lives of others. The Holy Spirit intends that this river cascade out from the hearts of all the faithful, and he intends to use the witness of each believer to extend the gracious rule of Christ, touching through each of us the lives of dozens, then hundreds, then countless people world-wide. The reformers of the 16th century called this concept, "the priesthood of all believers." (See 1 Pet 2:9–10.)

As Jesus has taught us, the church prays day by day, week by week, "Hallowed be thy name; thy kingdom come; thy will be done . . . ." In large measure, each of these petitions reflects the longing of God's heart that even as Christ died for all, so all would repent and "come to the knowledge of the truth" (1 Tim 2:4). This primary call, the call to faith and salvation, brings eternal purpose and meaning to our lives. But it does not bring "happiness" or peace as the world system around us would define them. Jesus repeatedly warned his followers:

> Do not suppose that I have come to bring peace to the earth. I did not come to bring peace, but a sword. . . . Anyone who loves his father or mother more than me is not worthy of me; anyone who loves his son or daughter more than me is not worthy of me; and

anyone who does not take his cross and follow me is not worthy of me. (Matt 10:34, 37–38; NIV)

I have told you these things, so that in me you may have peace. In this world you will have trouble. But take heart! I have overcome the world. (John 16:33; NIV)

The sword, the crosses of life, the troubles of which our Savior warned come because of the sin in our own hearts. They come because Satan prowls like a roaring lion, intending to devour us. They come because Satan and his demons influence the world system around us, using it to bring temptation, tribulation, and persecution into our lives.

To counter the destructive force of this "unholy trinity" (the world, our sinful nature, and Satan), God confers various callings on all the baptized, in addition to his call to faith. In these various "vocations," we as God's children serve the people around us and, in doing so, serve God's purposes for our world.[2] Governors and soldiers, mail room clerks and parents, doctors and traffic cops, writers, actors, and pastry chefs—all add to the order, joy, and harmony in our world and oppose the schemes of Satan by combating sickness, poverty, ugliness, violence, and need of every kind. All who pursue God's calling in their godly occupations and in what the reformers called "stations" (neighbors, parents, employees, etc.) do so under the blessing of God. This is the doctrine of vocation.

Furthermore, in mercy and concern that his people receive the spiritual care that will make it possible for them to grow up in the faith he has planted in us, the Holy Spirit calls some from among the priesthood of all believers to serve in the public ministry of his church. As with the call to faith, God's call to public service in his name does not derive from his concern for our "happiness" in some ephemeral, earthly sense. Rather, it derives from his concern for our ultimate "blessedness" and the ultimate "blessedness" of all his people. In answer to Christ's call to public ministry in his name, we lay down our rights and pick up our cross to follow our Lord.

To speak plainly and practically, for the sake of the call we set aside the privilege of eating our meals in peace and instead pick up the telephone when it rings with a request that we come to church or school right away on a matter of great (or, as it may sometimes turn out, minor) importance. For the sake of the call, we abandon the hope of retiring to a

2. In grace, God also uses the work of non-Christians in the service of his purposes here on earth. Two essays in this volume, "Teaching the Tension" and "Our Peculiar Ministry," describe God's "two strategies." That material, key to an understanding of this present chapter, will not be repeated here.

villa on some Grand Cayman seashore. For the sake of the call, we forego a prestigious job title and the power it could bring. For the sake of the call, we walk away from the personal privacy most Americans have come to expect, recognizing that the clothes we wear, the hobbies we choose, the car we drive, the conduct of our children—all these will become matters for public speculation and, on occasion, even criticism.

In accepting God's call to public ministry, we set out with Moses on a camping trip deep inside this world's wilderness, an excursion that may last perhaps four decades and more, a journey that will fill our sandals and sandwiches with sand and that will drain every last drop of energy and compassion we can muster for those we serve. With Moses, we move into our service realizing we will face every temptation common to the human race and also knowing we will face additional temptations, temptations unique to our calling as public servants of God's people. We move forward, knowing we will succumb at times to all of these temptations, and yet, trusting Christ's mercy to sustain and pardon us.

Blessedness!

So then, why go? Why obey? Why write that letter of acceptance, and in doing so let God place all this responsibility and all these potential burdens on our shoulders? As we begin to answer that, we note that Moses did in the end voluntarily head back to Egypt. He may have muttered to himself in fear and frustration for 500 miles at the thought of what might lie ahead, but God did not turn him into a "Stepford wife"; Moses was no robot made compliant by some kind of spiritual lobotomy. If the Lord refused to force Moses, he surely will not force us.

The God who calls us has the right to set us apart for whatever service, whatever vocation, he chooses. He has created and redeemed us and, thus, could coerce us as he coerced Pharaoh to let Israel go. Yahweh could demand and insist on our service. Yet, in gentleness, he does not do so. Instead, he asks. He "calls." He convinces us of the honor, the blessedness, the dignity, the meaning his call confers. One Christian hymn writer of another generation phrased part of the reason for our compliance with God's call to public ministry in the form of a prayer:

> As lab'rers in Thy vineyard, Lord, send us out to be
> Content to bear the burden of weary days for Thee,
> To ask no other wages when Thou shalt call us home
> Than to have shared the travail which makes Thy
> kingdom come. (John Monsell, 1866)

"Follow your passion?" No. Rather, follow the voice of your Savior whose will for your life is good and gracious. Follow the call he has so generously given, trusting his promise to bless you in your following. Instead of "happiness," our Savior calls us to "blessedness," to that same deep and satisfying contentment he himself experienced as he followed the call of his Father here on earth. This "blessedness" is the word Jesus himself used in the Beatitudes (Matt 5:1–11). Transliterated from the Greek as *makarios*, the word connotes having a characteristic in common with God. The New Testament uses this term to express "the distinctive joy which comes through participation in the divine kingdom."[3]

The call to public service in Christ's church for us, as for Christ, always brings blessedness, just as it also always involves a cross. The writer to the Hebrews describes our Savior's viewpoint on his Father's call and hints at our response to the crosses we ourselves carry as teachers in the church:

> Let us run with perseverance the race marked out for us. Let us fix our eyes on Jesus, the author and perfecter of our faith, *who for the joy set before him endured the cross, scorning its shame*, and sat down at the right hand of the throne of God. Consider him who endured such opposition from sinful men, so that you will not grow weary and lose heart. (Heb 12:1–3; NIV, *emphasis mine*)

Earlier, the holy writer described the effects this endurance created in Christ:

> For it was fitting that he, for whom and by whom all things exist, in bringing many sons to glory, should make the founder of their salvation perfect through suffering. (Heb 12:10; ESV)

Note the repetition of the word perfecter/perfect in each of these passages. The Greek root from which it derives carries the connotation of completion, of bringing something to its full consummation, its ultimate conclusion or perhaps even its absolute "destiny." Jesus endured the cross, looking forward to joy that would be his when our faith in the salvation he won for us would be complete and would unite us to himself forever. His suffering made the joy possible. The cross accomplished the complete salvation for which he yearned; as the writer to the Hebrews says, "Without the shedding of blood there is no forgiveness" (Heb 9:22; NIV).

---

3. *Theological Dictionary of the New Testament*, edited by G. Kittel; abridged (Grand Rapids, Mich: Eerdmans, 1985) 548.

As we serve our brothers and sisters in Jesus in myriad ways, helping them to grow up in their salvation, suffering intertwines integrally with the package. Paul put it this way:

> Now I rejoice in what was suffered for you and I fill up in my flesh what is still lacking in regard to Christ's afflictions, for the sake of his body, which is the church. I have become its servant by the commission God gave me to present to you the word of God in its fullness . . . (Col 1:24–25; NIV)

The children, youth, and adults we serve have one Savior. We are not him! Still, we endure hardships in ways similar to the apostle Paul as we fulfill our calling to "present the word of God in its fullness" to those we disciple. As we do this, we too grow in our own discipleship. We become more like our Savior, "learning obedience" (Heb 5:8) through the "light and momentary troubles" (2 Cor 4:17) we carry in our calling for Christ's people.

As we mature, we begin to see little interruptions, the lack of privacy, and even the financial burdens as minor. We trade these trivial worries for other burdens, burdens of more significance. Our hearts, for example, ache as we watch those we disciple make ungodly choices. We agonize in prayer for families caught up in a tangled mess of alcoholism or drug abuse. We sigh over unresolved conflict in our congregation, especially when the offenses that precipitate the conflict seem so petty. We watch in horror as someone who serves in public ministry beside us falls into gross sin. We feel frustration and disappointment as we find ourselves never quite able to live up to the expectations the members of this board or that parent places on us.

These and other burdens like them are the true crosses of the public ministry. We hurt and we become weary at times as we carry crosses like these. And yet, even as that happens, the Lord Jesus is at work within us through his Word. He applies that Word and the comfort of the Sacraments to the events of our lives, re-crafting our character and our personality in ways that make us more and more uniquely like himself:

> And we all, with unveiled face, beholding the glory of the Lord, are being transformed into the same image from one degree of glory to another. For this comes from the Lord who is the Spirit. (2 Cor 3:18; ESV)

Note the word "uniquely" in the previous paragraph. As we fulfill his call to public ministry and continue to grow in Christ-likeness, we grow more like ourselves at the same time, more like the true and singular individuals he created us to be from all eternity. C. S. Lewis talks about this in the last chapter of *Mere Christianity*, using these words to describe our transformation:

> The more we get what we now call "ourselves" out of the way and let him take us over, the more truly ourselves we become. There is so much of him that millions and millions of "little Christs," all different, will still be too few to express him fully. . . . The more I resist him and try to live on my own, the more I become dominated by my heredity and surroundings and natural desires. . . . It is when I turn to Christ, when I give myself up to his Personality, that I first begin to have a real personality of my own.

Even now, here in this life, we glimpse bits of evidence that this process is indeed taking place. We begin to find satisfaction in seeing a first grader cry tears of true repentance, and we feel true elation in being able to assure this little one of God's forgiveness in Christ's cross. We start to recognize the privilege that is ours in reminding our third graders that the ice cream bars they slurp to celebrate the successful completion of a unit on fractions come as a gift of the good Creator who has also given them the intellect to grasp and apply mathematical concepts. We begin to experience genuine thankfulness for the peace God gives us in being able to pray with a youth group member for a friend dying of cancer. We grow in awareness that besides simply listening to the parent who has just lost his job, we can also share God's powerful Word of promise and assault the throne of grace with prayer on that parent's behalf.

These privileges, this blessedness, serve as a foretaste of the eternal feast to come and provide a down payment on our Savior's promise:

> Therefore, my dear brothers, stand firm. Let nothing move you. Always give yourselves fully to the work of the Lord, because you know that your labor in the Lord is not in vain. (I Cor 15:58; NIV)

But How Do I Decide?

Kurt Lewin, a respected social psychologist of the twentieth century, has noted, "There's nothing so practical as a good theory." Knowing what God is up to—in Christ, in his world, in his church, and in us as individuals—we can more easily make decisions when we face specific choices about where and how to serve him and his people. Shall I continue to teach? or should I serve in administration, organizing programs and supporting other faculty? Shall I teach in Peoria, Illinois? or in Peoria, Kansas? Is it God's will that I teach full-time in a Christian school? or should I direct youth and music programs in my home congregation, supporting myself, in part, by working at Wal-Mart?

To answer specific questions like these, we first need to recognize that our Lord can use any of his people in any of several key ways, perhaps in dozens or even hundreds of locations. Just as there is no one "right" spouse or no one "right" house or apartment for most of us, so there is in most cases no one "right" call.

Some Christian theologies propose that our Lord has only one best path for each believer. They teach that if we fail to find it or blatantly rebel against it, refusing to go where he sends us, we will then spend the rest of our lives in the salt marshes of his will, never quite able to fulfill the potential the Holy Spirit intended for us. What pressure this can put on a person to make that one "right" choice!

But how untrue! We need not fear somehow "missing the will of God" as we make decisions about his call on our lives. As we have seen, Moses committed murder. A very bad decision! Jonah clearly knew God's will—and ran 500 miles in the opposite direction. Another very bad decision. Yet Yahweh brought both prophets back on track and then used both of them mightily for the good of his people. Of course, we are not free to commit homicide, as did Moses. Nor would we want to walk away from tasks our Lord has clearly assigned to us, as Jonah tried to do.

Yet we do well to realize that God wants us to mature in Christlikeness. Because this is so, he refrains from dictating our every move. He orders our lives so that we operate within very broad boundaries of freedom in the Gospel of our Lord Jesus. But just as adult children sometimes consult their parents, talking over important decisions and asking for advice, so too we can talk to our heavenly Father. When we struggle with important decisions about serving God's people, we can ask him to do for us what he has promised:

> Delight yourself in the LORD, and he will give you the desires of your heart. (Ps 37:4; ESV)

While some have read the phrase, "the desires of your heart," to encompass material blessings like a red Corvette parked in the driveway or a mansion complete with billiard parlor and heated indoor pool, the rest of Scripture would point us back instead to "the *makarios* of God" and to the Spirit's work of conforming our hearts and desires to those of our Savior. As we mature, we learn to know Jesus better and better. We grow, as did

Christ, in "wisdom and stature" (Luke 2:52), becoming more and more like him, more and more fully ourselves in the eternal sense. As God works this in us, then Christ's desires become more and more fully our desires, too. We feel more and more deeply Jesus' concern for the good of others, both here on earth and in eternity.

If our Lord wants to use us in a specific place at a specific time to do specific things (and on occasion, he might—see, for example, Acts 8:26 ff), we can trust the Lord of the church to put us where he wants us to be. He can arrange our circumstances or use the counsel of other people or create a powerful desire in our hearts or even perform a miracle in the biblical sense—or all four—to move us into the lives of those among whom he wants to do that.

On the other hand, we also need to remember that it may not matter to the Holy Spirit in which Peoria we decide to teach. If two congregations have extended Calls, we may in faith exercise our freedom to move to Kansas or to stay in Illinois. Assuming our ministry will be productive in either place, our Savior may encourage us to choose for ourselves. As we do that, we thank him for his kindness in providing two options, for respecting our personhood, and for caring about our professional growth.

With this, then, as background, here are some practical approaches many called workers have found helpful:

- Sometimes making a list of clear pros and cons for each option will clarify one's thinking. (Remember, if you're already serving in a congregation and receive a call from another congregation, you have at that point two calls—one to your current service and one to the new situation.) Weighting the list, adding more points to facets of each position that matter most, can help you clarify further. Remember, God can work through circumstances—he did send a great fish to re-direct Jonah's path, for example. You need not consider yourself somehow "unspiritual" for asking the question: "What are my circumstances saying?" But even as you ask, remember that Moses saw God's "sign" after, not before, Israel was safely out of Egypt.

- Seek counsel. Talk with people who know you well, people who care about you, people who have saturated their minds and hearts in the Scriptures and who share your understanding of what it means to serve God's people in full-time ministry in his church. Ask them to pray with you and for you.

- Get away for a few days to slow down, to reflect, pray, read Scripture, and perhaps even fast for a time. A friend tells me he has sat on occasion for a day or two in a cemetery, reminding himself of his own mortality and considering his decision in the light of eternity. Some people take off to camp and meditate in a state park or national forest. I've used Christian retreat centers and inexpensive motels each to good advantage at various times for personal get-aways. Each has its own benefits and drawbacks, but either can work well as a sanctuary for thought and prayer if, that is, one can avoid the temptation to turn on the television or radio!

- Remember, Jesus doesn't always call us to do the hardest thing. Nor does he always call us to do the easiest thing. The lowest salary isn't necessarily a "sign" from heaven, nor is the longest summer vacation. On the other hand, if one particular set of circumstances will condemn you to perpetual indebtedness, think twice as you consider Rom 13:8 and the principle set down there for living within our means.

- In most situations, one's current call takes precedence. This means that if another congregation or institution extends a call, in general we should stay to fulfill our current call unless our deliberations clearly lead us to the conclusion the Lord wants to move us on into the new ministry site, the new opportunities for service.

Follow our passion? No. It's a far, far better thing to which Jesus invites us. He says to us instead, "Follow me!" What an awesome adventure to follow that call to teach in his church, to share his love with his people and with those who will, through us, become his people! Think of it! Christ's love, our response:

> Drawn to the cross, which thou hast blest
> With healing gifts for souls distressed,
> To find in thee my life, my rest,
> Christ Crucified, I come.
>
> And then for work to do for thee,
> Which shall so sweet a service be
> That angels well might envy me,
> Christ Crucified, I come.
>
> —Genevieve M. Irons

12

The Employerization of the Teaching Ministry

Russ Moulds

This chapter discusses several challenges the teaching ministry faces as the church's teachers consider their present and future identity.

T ODAY'S TEACHER in the Lutheran elementary school hardly thinks of herself or himself as an independent teacher of the church. She typically sees herself as a congregation member whose vocation includes teaching students in a Christian environment. So, too, the DCE, the professor in the Lutheran university, and the instructor in the Lutheran high school—these Christians perceive their teaching as being, in some sense, agents of an educational effort sponsored by or related to a congregation or a larger church body. But in the early church, being an independent church teacher was a common practice. This early church practice prompts certain questions about the vocational status of today's teachers and whether they are employees, self-employed, professionals, ministers, independent contractors, guild members, or yet some other sort of worker.

The most famous such independent church teacher was Origen (c.185–c. 254), a highly respected though not uncontroversial Bible teacher who conducted his classes in Alexandria, Egypt, and later in Caesarea, Palestine. Origen was the son of Christian parents. His mother was an Egyptian, and his father was a Roman centurion. His father was martyred in the imperial persecution in 202 but not before instructing Origen carefully in Scripture and doctrine. Because all the other Christian teachers had fled the persecution in Alexandria, young Origen was among the few remaining educated believers and stepped in to teach Christianity and Greek to adult catechumens.

Origen's teaching skills were evident from the start, and he attracted large numbers of students to Christianity as the persecution ebbed. In a few years he was well known in and out of the church, even instructing governors and members of the emperor's family, yet choosing to live a simple, ascetic life without need of much teaching income. Despite his growing fame and the success of his books, he continued to teach beginners in the Christian faith. Eventually Bishop Demitrius of Alexandria, envious of his teaching stature and spurred by petty jealousy, made Origen no longer welcome in Alexandria. Origen, always a lay teacher, then affiliated himself with the church at Caesarea, accepted ordination, and finished his teaching ministry there, dying of prolonged injuries from torture in another persecution that raged from 249 to 251 (McKechnie, 2001, p. 184).

Employer/Employee

Why this story about an ancient teacher for readers today? Clearly we are not independent teachers of the church as Origen was. What sort of teachers we are, however, is not so clear, and Origen's story helps us reflect on this ambiguous status. The thesis of this chapter is that Christian teachers, particularly Lutheran educators, are now chiefly (though not only) identified according to the modern category of employee and that, while this characterization has some limited use, it should be minimized. Let's look first at the evidence for this category of teacher-as-employee along with reasons for concern. Next I'll make a case for why we should avoid characterizing the church teacher as an employee. Finally, I'll close with some suggestions for maintaining teacher identity without being too strident about the need for remedy.

The employer/employee relationship refers to a modern labor model in which a person sells her or his labor to another under conditions determined by the other with those conditions constrained at least minimally by laws and interests of the state. The model understands that the employee owns his labor and the employer owns the conditions and resources for how the worker's labor is employed (or, from the original Latin word, involved). While not perfect, the model is a largely successful approach to labor relations in a market economy. Despite its practicality, it's a model we should not use for the church worker. Yet we cast the church teacher as an employee in a number of conspicuous and subtle ways. As we consider those ways, consider also the tension between the two kingdoms and our need to work with both of God's strategies as discussed in chapters 3 and 4.

The Teacher as Employee

One way by which congregations, their schools, and their church bodies increasingly regard church teachers as employees is through the use of contracts rather than calls. The recent history of this practice is mixed and complex. Call practice is the prerogative of the congregation, and they may exercise this practice, including contracts, in any way that is not clearly contrary to Scripture.[1] Synodical institutions such as districts and colleges have regarded their workers' positions as contingent and not defined by the enduring call conditions of a congregation. However, a contract characterizes the worker's relationship in terms of Law rather than Gospel. It gives an institution the latitude to eliminate positions when the budget shrinks, and does so in a way that regards the teacher as a commodity rather than partner in the Gospel (Phil 1:5). What's more, it creates a culture in which the church worker can be dismissed by non-renewal of a contract rather than a process of mutual Christian conversation and consolation to assist and perhaps re-direct that person's ministry. Contracts are efficient, expedient, and legal. Calls are sloppy, personal, and evangelical. As we see the proliferation of search committees rather than call committees, we see the contract culture grow among us.[2]

The business and benefit offices which assist the material welfare of church workers now customarily refer to teachers as employees. These offices must manage the paperwork of outside agencies such as insurance companies that operate with corporate and business world views and terminology. Trying to function with two sets of terms—employee and minister—is confusing, and referring to teachers as employees is a reasonable simplification in working with these organizations. In fact, one constant source of confusion is the IRS which simultaneously treats church teachers as self-employed workers, employees with W-2 forms, and ministers of the Gospel. The point here is not to argue for consistency and clarity among

1. For example, The Lutheran Church–Missouri Synod Council of Presidents of the synodical districts has encouraged use of the call rather than contracts for rostered church workers in its document, "Rubrics Governing Call and Placement Procedures," adopted in its April, 2002, meeting. Copies are available through links from www.lcms.org.

2. Search committees are common practice in business, higher education, and non-profit organizations seeking to fill professional positions. In this practice, the conditions of employment are negotiated and often defined by a contract. Many church bodies today use a search-and-contract approach to secure workers. It is instructive to recall that Jesus did not issue contracts to his disciples (though such arrangements did exist in biblical times). For a biblically informed discussion of the divine call see D. R. Koehneke, "The Call Into the Holy Ministry" in *The Abiding Word*, edited by T. Laetsch (St. Louis: Concordia Publishing House, 1946).

the powers and principalities of the world. The point is that we in the church, though also in the world, should be cautious about subscribing blithely to the world's models and terms (Eph 5:15) even as we must make use of them. Notice here the tension of the two kingdoms discussed in chapters 3 and 4.

Another considerable influence on employerization of the teaching ministry is our necessary attention to school law and tort law. In our litigious society, every church, church agency, and church school must now be prepared to face legal challenges, civil and criminal. We are a nation of laws, these laws are written to address our society and economy, and we are a society and economy of employers and employees. Just as dealing with business and government agencies outside the church has its impact on our identity, so dealing with criminal claims and law suits takes its toll on how we are perceived, our self-perception, and the biblical terms and models with which we describe ourselves.

The teaching ministry also shares some degree of relationship with the government's interest in public education, and this contributes to our employee culture. Some of these relationships are formal while others are superficial. Within the doctrine of the two kingdoms and our two strategies, we recognize the state's compelling interest in health standards and criminal conduct in the church's affairs. We share a relative though not absolute interest in standards regarding any temporal curriculum we may convey in the classroom. More superficially, some of our pedagogical conduct is like some of the behaviors of teachers in public (and private) schools and universities, just as some of a pastor's actions look like the behavior of a motivational speaker, politician, sales representative, or office manager. But a teacher of the church can no more be compared to government school teachers than a pastor of the church can be compared to a public health administrator. Similar as some of their features may be, the natures and purposes of their activities are two different worlds or kingdoms apart. However, the frequent public school teacher comparison reinforces the employee perception.

This limited relationship and intersection with some of society's involvement in education includes attention to present-day interests in accreditation and accreditation agencies. The concepts and practices of accreditation are of value in some ways for the church's use of education as a vehicle for outreach. Accreditation is one means for alerting those outside our circles that we pursue excellence in our service (since, of course, we would do no less for our King; see Phil 4:8 and 1 Pet 2:12). Accreditation, however, can take on an excessive and even defining influence for the teaching ministry of our schools. The agencies themselves are generally accommodating toward a church school or university's religious nature. More disconcerting is the school's preoccupation with and devotion of time and resources to the subsidiary task of accreditation rather than our primary mission in the Gospel. This preoccupation with an interest that belongs to the public domain further identifies teaching in the church with employment rather than ministry.[3]

Offices and titles comprise another preoccupation that inclines the teaching ministry toward employerization. Like the poor, offices and titles will always be with us. They're part of our being in the world. They do, in fact, serve the limited purpose of identifying a person with a certain role in some aspect of one's calling, and this is an organizational convenience for those seeking or in need of service. But, after Eden, just as money is not merely a means of exchange, and grades are not merely a measure of learning, offices and titles have taken on superfluous significance, signifying more than mere function for the well-being of one's neighbor. Teaching in the church is rank with titles, but this evidence for employerization is subtle and will require some scrutiny.

Titles and offices have been part of the church from the beginning, and Scripture contains several roles and offices such as deacon (table waiter), pastor (shepherd), and presbyter (elder), some of them established by God (Eph 4:11), and others invented by the church (Acts 6:1ff).[4] The biblical context of these and other roles indicates clearly the foot-washing posture of the office-holder.

Here again, the point is not to dismiss or even denigrate titles. If we eliminated one set of titles, we would eventually replace it with another out of need for communicating about our vocations. And, not to overstate the point, titles are not universally a matter of superiority and lording it over others. In many of our settings, we serve effectively and mutually within a flexible organizational chart. The point is that we now seem more and more to attach to titles and offices an importance of human custom and esteem not found in a context of the Gospel.

3. The National Lutheran Schools Accreditation program seeks to assist Lutheran schools with an accreditation process that both sustains the school's spiritual integrity and meets the criteria of regional accrediting agencies. See the NLSA website at http://dcs. lcms.org.

4. See "Theology and Practice of 'the Divine Call,'" a report of the Commission on Theology and Church Relations (St. Louis: Lutheran Church-Missouri Synod, 2004), or see the CTCR web page at www.lcms.org.

My observation about title and office is not an empirical research claim, but neither is it mere idiosyncracy. Consider some of the titles in use within the teaching ministry today and whether they communicate that posture of foot-washing: headmaster, director of ministries, executive director, chief executive officer, department chair, provost, principal, and the assistant, associate, and full ranks of professor. The local reality, of course, depends on the Christian character of whoever occupies the office. But our language is now characterized more by notions of careerism and professionalism than by taking up a cross and being the servant and slave (Mark 10:35–45). The assumption—now often spoken rather than unspoken—is that we ought to aspire to certain offices and positions, an assumption out of keeping with Luke 14:1–24, 1 Cor 7:17–24, and the biblical doctrine of vocation. As we orient more toward this language of careerism and professionalism rather than the language of the cross, our theology of the cross shifts toward a theology of glory, and we re-orient to employerization rather than calling and vocation.[5]

Consider one more set of evidence with both some subtle and conspicuous elements. The current proliferation of literature, conferences, and buzzwords about leadership is now very much part of the Christian education scene. The leadership theme within the church is provoked in part by the shortage of both pastors and administrators for church education. While the need and concern for filling these offices is genuine, emphasis on this leadership theme is over-pronounced and tends to eclipse the biblical role of the *didaskalos*, the teacher of the church (1 Cor 12:28–29; Eph 4:11; James 3:1).[6] The concept of leadership may in some sense be implicit in any biblical role (or any role or office we as a church may fashion) but is not, like *didaskalos*, itself an explicit vocational theme in Scripture. And an explicit emphasis on leadership, largely drawn from business and management literature, tends to project employerization into the teaching ministry. This emphasis on leadership also tends to create a climate of

5. A recent illustration in my own ministry appears in a memo from a college dean's office regarding a possible contract to a Lutheran high school educator: "He has worked his way up through the system, having come from _____ Lutheran High School as a teacher." This cultural characteristic of career aspiration in church ministry deserves further attention than space allows. Luther addressed it in his setting when writing about "the sneak preachers" (*im winkel*). See *Luther's Works*, St. Louis ed. (20:1665ff). Luther also addressed it in his essay on calling teachers. See *Luther's Works*, St. Louis edition (10:1543–44).

6. The New Testament Greek word for teacher is *didaskalos*. Its use and meaning has been the subject of much discussion about church offices and functions. Treatments of the word can be found in Bible lexicons and word books such as A. Richardson, *A Theological Word Book of the Bible* (Macmillan, 1950).

hierarchy common in employment contexts but inappropriate in the work of the church. Two indications of this climate include some applications of policy-based governance and some curious anomalies in salary.

Policy-based governance refers to focusing the work of the board of directors on mission, goals, and policies rather than their micro-managing the organization's operations. In Christian education, this approach is feasible and desirable provided the board understands itself as a steward of the church's mission and servant to the teachers of the church (who are servants to those they teach). Misapplication of this governance model happens when the board isolates itself from the ministration of the church's teachers and invents some new teaching mission for which teachers are then deputized as subordinate agents.[7]

A second indication of a shift toward leadership as hierarchy rather than the inverted and emptying pattern Paul preached (and practiced) in Phil 2:1–11 is the disproportionate executive-style salary not uncommon in the church today. Synodical officers, university administrators, and some high school and elementary school administrators receive compensation for their activities on behalf of the Gospel disturbingly out of proportion to their fellow slaves of Christ.[8] The point here is not to invoke some sort of egalitarian reform—which would soon collapse in our condition of *simul iustus et peccator* (at the same time justified and sinful). Besides, individual office holders can always practice humble stewardship with however few or many temporal blessings are entrusted to them. The point is that our practice and pattern in this ministry to which we are yoked in common (Matt 11:28–30) looks conspicuously hierarchical and worldly in the cases of some very conspicuous offices. This corporate executive modeling contributes to a culture of employerization and does so in an era of Enron and other corporate abuses of stakeholders. What's more, it emulates and

7. I am not sounding an anti-administration charge, though some may so mis-read my meaning. I am noticing that the way we communicate about the significance of various roles and offices will take on a certain frame of reference, and we need to consider how harmonious this frame of reference is with Scripture. The aim is not to come up with pure and perfect expressions but to select words and themes that are approximately congruent with our convictions. Regarding teachers of the church as employees lacks this congruence.

8. A biblical rationale for these disproportionate salaries is not obvious. Perspectives include the belief that we would never get anyone to accept these positions and their tasks without such salaries; that those with the skills to hold these positions deserve these salaries; and that these offices are commensurate with similar positions in the domains of public education, business, government, and non-profit organizations, and we ought to stay competitive with them.

ratifies the sort of worldly conduct in the church that the Reformation repudiated five centuries ago.

Does It Matter?

No single point above makes the case that we have subverted or displaced the ministry of teaching by turning that ministry into the occupation of a commercial, civil, or non-profit organization. Cumulatively, however, these several conditions for teaching in the church now make for a climate, culture, and context of market economy employment rather than the biblical tradition of a calling to ministry. Does it matter?

It does matter because how we regard and portray the ministry of the church is one tangible way that God has given us to communicate the distinctiveness of the Gospel. Maintaining that distinction matters because God has spoken a Word of grace and promise into this world which abides and works in this world but remains apart from it. That Word must remain both in, yet apart from, the world so that its Good News of our being reconciled with God through Christ can be present and lively among us but not confused with any message or news contrived within this fallen creation. Our ministry of this Word is no sort of employment of education, information, or news invented by this world. For this reason, the Reformers insisted that the Word we share is a Word "external" to the institutions, orders, realms, powers, and principalities of this world. It is even external to the church itself (Luke 1:35; Matt 16:17; Acts 2:2, 17) and is not the creation or possession of its offices (John 3:5–8). Employment is activity in the temporal labor of the kingdom of this world. Ministry is activity in the eternal Word of the kingdom of heaven.

Yet we need to be careful about how we say that this distinction from employment matters. If we say it in a way that denigrates the temporal employment and occupation of our fellow Christians, we imply that the earthly labors of their jobs and professions are not part of their vocation as Christians—and that is false. The honest labor of every Christian is part of the way God sustains the world he so loves "that he sent his only begotten Son." The first article of the Apostles' Creed reminds us that through these employments, God provides "food and clothing, home and family, and all I need from day to day." Distinguishing the ministry of teaching from employment does not create first- and second-class Christians. It serves to keep the Gospel as God's Good News for the world rather than just another notion about God from the world.

We also need to be careful not to imply that a teacher of the church is somehow more sanctified or valued by God than those employed in occupations and professions in the world. Earlier I contrasted church teachers and pastors with public educators and public health administrators. The contrast is not between the eternal value of the persons in different offices or the honor of their activities. The contrast is between the temporal affairs of this world and the eternal promises of God's kingdom that Christians in all vocations have and share. We have already distinguished the temporal and eternal in the two kingdoms doctrine (chapters 3 and 4), remembering that both strategies—the "left" and the "right"—are God's.

Teaching in the church, then, belongs to the biblical tradition of the calling to ministry. We have affirmed this by seeing how distinguishing it from employment preserves and accentuates the Gospel but doesn't create special status for the person who is teaching. The distinction then, for the sake of the Gospel, implies these sorts of relationship principles, principles that are well established in the New Testament and already worked out in previous discussions:[9]

- Teaching in the church portrays a different kingdom than does employment in our market economy, and we seek to distinguish and not confuse those two kingdoms (John 17:13–20).
- The teacher of the church does not sell her or his ministry of the Gospel in the labor market, but does receive a living from those who benefit by that teaching (Matt 10:10; 1 Cor 9:14).
- The relationship of the teacher to the Christian community, while informed by the Law, is characterized by the Gospel and not regulated by the Law and manifestations of the Law such as contracts (Rom 6–8; Gal 2–4; 1 Cor 9).[10]
- The teacher of the church does not participate in a hierarchy (from the Greek, *hiero + arche*, sacred rulers, referring to some organization of ascending holy ranks and offices). Rather, the teacher is one among sisters and brothers in Christ who conducts the office of teacher on behalf of these other Christians.

9. Walther elaborates several theses about the ministry of the church and addresses several principles and concepts that can inform a Biblical outlook in the Lutheran tradition about employment and ministry. See Walther, *Church and Ministry*.

10. Shortly after the Reformation, the issue of contracts was already a lively topic. Jerome Kromayer (1610–1670) in his book, *Theology Pro and Con*, argued against contracts in the ministry. See "Rubrics Governing Call and Placement Procedures" (The Lutheran Church–Missouri Synod; April, 2002).

- The teacher of the church is not a hireling. The office of the teacher is an office of the Gospel itself, and it reflects the nature and character of the Good Shepherd who is also called Rabbi (see John 10:7–18).[11]

Changing Direction

Life, including life in the church, is sloppy. However precisely we write our doctrines and interpretations, our applications are never very precise. Nevertheless, the kingdom of God will still come, it will come for us, and that's a relief. So rather than summing up our discussion with several strident correctives, a few suggestions will do better. Better to be headed in the right direction, however erratic, than to remain stuck in place trying to fix everything first.

I think our current tendency toward employerization is the wrong direction. We could change that direction by avoiding contracts for teachers whenever possible. Congregation pastors and district officials could speak out about this a bit more. They could help school boards and personnel committees consider whether they are motivated more by fear of "getting stuck with a lemon" than by a spirit of trust and hope, and under what unusual conditions a contract might be appropriate.

We could change direction by providing some instruction about the two kingdoms. We who teach may be remiss in not helping Christians to better understand how the kingdoms are different, how they are related, and how the Christian must live simultaneously in both. Helping them to understand this can help them appreciate their congregation's ministry and their own priestly ministry. We could also avoid the public school teacher comparison while endorsing the vocation of public educators in God's kingdom of the left.

We could change direction by occasionally reminding ourselves and our business offices that, though we must sometimes use the language of business, our ministers are not employees. A gentle word, an insertion in a bulletin, or a brief and pleasant memo from time to time would probably be enough. Similarly, we could recognize that we must and should interact with the institutions of this world but be careful not to grant them peremptory status. Accreditation agencies, state departments of education, legal claimants, and other entities of the left-handed kingdom have an

11. C. F. W. Walther, *Church and Ministry: The Witness of the Evangelical Lutheran Church on the Question of Church and Ministry* (St. Louis: Concordia Publishing House, 1987) 205, 207, 305.

ancillary role in some of our activities. Our identity and priorities, established by God's Word, are already located in other larger concerns. Again, a gentle reminder from time to time would help.

And we could change direction by emphasizing the *didaskalos* commitments of the teaching ministry rather than offices, titles, and leadership. Those we entrust with our operational activities such as budgets, supplies, schedules, and planning perform essential duties that are critical to our ministry in today's world, and for them we give thanks to God. Yet these fellow servants are not our leaders—for we have only one Master and Teacher (Matt 23:8–12). While this re-emphasis may at first sound peculiar, iconoclastic, and unrealistic, any cursory review of how the Lutheran tradition has hammered out these ideas over the last five hundred years will confirm a healthy caution toward officialdom.[12]

Conclusion

Origen, that independent teacher of the early church, cannot be our model for today. Neither can the sixteenth century Lutheran school teachers and professors in Wittenberg who functioned both as civil servants and as ministers of the church. We learn from them that they were shaped by their times. But they were also shaped by deliberately engaging their theology with those times, and this yielded effective teaching for the church then.

We in our time will have to work out our salvation with our share of fear and trembling (Phil 2:12). Meanwhile, I have not here worked out a definition and explication of the teacher of the church for today. I haven't addressed the terminology and nomenclature questions about teachers and the office of the ministry. I have only said that if we are not working out what *didache* (the act of teaching Christians) means today, we will continue to be shaped only by our times and not also by our faith and theological tradition. Meanwhile, teachers are not employees. We can take that one off the list. Now we can consider other possibilities.

---

12. Luther, in his *Treatise on Secular Authority: To What Extent It Should Be Obeyed*, explains at length why hierarchy, authority of office, and ranking should not be practiced among Christians. One of the functions of the two kingdom doctrine is to serve as a check on human and worldly powers, remind us that they are penultimate, and keep them subordinate to God's ultimate authority and activity—including and sometimes especially in the church.

Epilogue
Some Concluding Prepositions

JAMES H. PRAGMAN

This epilogue invites readers to reflect on the preceding chapters
and continue to form and perhaps reform their understanding
of what it means to be a teacher of the church.

A Teacher of the Church
A Teacher for the Church
A Teacher in the Church
A Teacher from the Church
A Teacher with the Church
A Teacher to the Church

PREPOSITIONS ARE important. One could write the theology of the
church on the basis of the prepositions used to describe the church's
life and work.

The preposition *for* helps Lutherans understand themselves and helps
other Christians understand Lutherans: Lutherans teach, believe, and confess that Christ came into this world at the Father's bidding to suffer and
die and rise again *for* us and *for* our justification and *for* our salvation.
Christ came *for* us! That is bedrock Lutheran (and biblical!) theology!

This book's title uses the preposition *of*: "A Teacher *of* the Church."
That little preposition can denote many facets of a thing's meaning, but
perhaps it would not be too wide of the mark to suggest that the preposition in the title of this book suggests ownership and possession. The
teacher we are talking about belongs to the church and, consequently,
serves the church. The job of the teacher, if we may put it that way, is
to speak the truth of the church, the truth that the church is called to
expound, explain, and exhibit in all its doings. Thus, the teacher is *of* the
church.

But the teacher is also *for* the church and *in* the church and *from* the church and *with* the church and *to* the church. The teacher—whatever the context of teacher's activity—is there for the welfare of the church, to remind the church of its calling and its confession and its proclamation of the Lord's truth. The teacher lives and works for the sake of the church, to insure that the church lives up to its calling as the bride of Christ and His presence in the world.

The teacher comes from within the church to shape the church itself and to call the church to faithfulness in its servanthood before the Lord and the world. The teacher learns the doctrine revealed in the Bible and strategizes accordingly. Thus, as Melanchthon reminds us, all of Scripture should be divided into the two chief doctrines of Law and Gospel.[1] This book challenges us to consider what it means to be a teacher *from* the church who understands and rightly divides Law and Gospel in the divine calling of being a teacher.

The teacher never is alone as teacher: the teacher is surrounded by learners and supervisors and constituents and members and communities. The teacher is of the church and in the church and for the church and also *with* the church as it pushes forward its task and calling as witness to Christ and proclaimer of Law and Gospel to a world that has little interest in either. The church is support for the teacher, and the teacher *from* the church speaks to a larger world that may or may not be listening. But the teaching must happen for the sake of the world and for Christ's sake.

The teacher is also one who speaks *to* the church. The church—as its history demonstrates so obviously—is always in need of reformation, and that is true for every generation of the church. The church as our fathers experienced it Sunday after Sunday no longer exists; our experience of the church is much different than theirs. Nevertheless, we take what we have learned from those fathers in order to apply the received gift to our new circumstances and situations. As this book makes clear, the church's connection with culture is complex and challenging. And when that work is on the verge of wearing us down, we need to remember what we have heard in other contexts: "Ain't nothin' easy!"—especially in the calling of being a teacher. And yet, the work is that of the Lord who accomplishes his purposes in the midst of challenges and opportunities that are the domain of the teacher. He is courage and power and joy and peace for teacher and student alike.

1. "The Apology of the Augsburg Confession," in *The Book of Concord: The Confessions of the Evangelical Lutheran Church*, edited by Robert Kolb and Timothy J. Wengert (Minneapolis: Fortress Press, 2000) 121.5 [IV.5].

Are teachers employees or more than that? Yes! Are the challenges daunting or exhilarating? Yes! Are the joys full or incomplete? Yes! Are the strategies obvious or hidden? Yes! But the truth is clear. What fails us are the words we use to proclaim the Word God has spoken. And yet, the all-too-human teacher of the church receives the call and the calling to teach and shape and form and challenge and learn.

It is the hope of those who have contributed to this volume of essays that you as the reader will use this book to help you reflect on what it means to be a teacher of the church. We hope also that this book will challenge you to think about what it means to participate in both church and world in the teaching enterprise.

Don't forget the prepositions!

Bibliography

Althaus, Paul. *The Theology of Martin Luther*. Philadelphia: Fortress Press, 1966.

Benne, Robert. *Ordinary Saints*. Philadelphia: Fortress Press, 1988.

Braaten, Carl. *Principles of Lutheran theology*. Minneapolis: Fortress Press, 1983.

Christensen, Tom. *The Gift and Task of Lutheran Higher Education*. Minneaspolis: Augsburg Fortress, 2004.

Dillenberger, John. *God Hidden and Revealed*. Philadelphia: Muhlenberg Press, 1953.

————, translator. *Martin Luther: Selections from his Writings*. New York: Anchor Books, 1962.

Fenstermacher, G. D. and J. F. Soltis. *Approaches to Teaching*. New York: Teachers College Press, 1986.

Graebner, Theodore. *The Borderland of Right and Wrong*. St. Louis: Concordia Publishing House, 1953.

Harran, Marilyn. *Martin Luther: Learning for Life*. St. Louis: Concordia Publishing House, 1997.

Hartwig, Raymond. "Contemporary Issues Regarding the Universal Priesthood," in *Church and Ministry*. St. Louis: Concordia Publishing House, 1998.

Hauerwas, Stanley and William Willimon. *Resident Aliens: Life in the Christian Colony*. Knoxville, Tenn: Abingdon Press, 1989.

Jenkins, Phillip. *The Next Christendom*. New York: Oxford University Press, 2002.

Klos, Frank W. *Confirmation and First Communion: A Study Book*. Minneapolis, Philadelphia, and St. Louis: Augsburg Publishing House, Board of Publication of the Lutheran Church in America, and Concordia Publishing House, 1968.

Klug, Eugene. *Church and Ministry*. St. Louis: Concordia Publishing House, 1986.

Kolb, Robert. *The Christian faith: A Lutheran Exposition*. St. Louis: Concordia Publishing House, 1993.

Laetsch, Theodore, editor. *The Abiding Word: An Anthology of Doctrinal Essays*. 3 Vol. St. Louis: Concordia Publishing House, 1946–1960.

Luther, Martin. *The Bondage of the Will*, translated by J. I. Packer and O. R. Johnson. Grand Rapids. Mich: Fleming H. Revell, 1957.

————. *Luther's Works*, American Edition. St. Louis: Concordia Publishing House, 1986.

MacIntyre, Alasdair. *After virtue*. Notre Dame, Ind.: Notre Dame University Press, 1981.

McGrath, Alister. *Luther's Theology of the Cross*. Oxford: Blackwell, 1985.

McKechnie, Paul. *The First Christian Centuries: Perspectives on the Early Church*. Downers Grove, Ill: Intervarsity Press, 2001.

Menuge, A. J. L., editor. *Christ and Culture in Dialogue*. St. Louis: Concordia Publishing House, 1999.

Mueller, Steven P., editor. *Called to Believe, Teach, and Confess: An Introduction to Doctrinal Theology*. Eugene, Ore.: Wipf & Stock Publishers, 2005.

Nafzger, Samuel. *An Introduction to The Lutheran Church–Missouri Synod*. St. Louis: Concordia Publishing House, 1994.

Bibliography

Nafzger, Samuel. "The Called and Ordained Servant of the Lord and the Priesthood of All Believers." A paper delivered at the Nebraska District Pastoral Conference, Feb. 8, 1999.

Naisbitt, John and Patricia Aburdene. *Megatrends 2000*. New York: William Morrow and Company, 1990.

Oberman, Heiko. *Luther: Man between God and the Devil*. New York: Image, 1992.

Pragman, James H. *Traditions of Ministry: A History of the Doctrine of The Ministry in Lutheran Theology*. St. Louis: Concordia Publishing House, 1983.

"Spiritual Gifts: A Report of the Commission on Theology and Church Relations." St. Louis: The Lutheran Church–Missouri Synod, 1995.

Spitz, L. W. "The Universal Priesthood of Believers," *The Abiding Word*, Vol. I. St. Louis: Concordia Publishing House, 1946.

Tappert, Theodore. *The Book of Concord*. Philadelphia: Fortress Press, 1959.

Veith, Gene E. *The Spirituality of the Cross: The Way of the First Evangelicals*. St. Louis: Concordia Publishing House, 1999.

Walther, C. F. W. *The Proper Distinction Between Law and Gospel* (Translated by W. H. T. Dau). St. Louis: Concordia Publishing House, 1986. (Other translations and abridgements are available.)

Wingren, Gustaf. *Luther on Vocation*. Philadelphia: Muhlenberg Press, 1957.

Suggested Reading

THESE SELECTIONS will help the reader gain an increased scope of the history, practice, theology, and Christian thought related to teaching in the church. Some of the readings are polemic and argue a particular position. Others provide more general background that can inform the teaching ministry. They cover a range of settings across congregations, schools, and higher education. Many are Lutheran in orientation, but some sources provide perspectives from other traditions. Most have been widely read at one time or another and have shaped past and present views about what it means to be a teacher of the church.

Christenson, Tom. *The Gift and Task of Lutheran Higher Education*. Minneapolis: Augsburg Fortress, 2004.

Commission on Theology and Church Relations. *The Ministry: Offices, Procedures, and Nomenclature*. St. Louis: The Lutheran Church–Missouri Synod, 1981.

———. *Theology and Practice of the Divine Call*. St. Louis: The Lutheran Church–Missouri Synod, 2003.

Dillenberger, John, editor. *Martin Luther: Selections from His Writings*. New York: Anchor Doubleday, 1962.

Fryar, Jane L. *Go and Make Disciples: The Goal of the Christian Teacher*. St. Louis: Concordia Publishing House, 1992.

Harran, Marilyn. *Martin Luther: Learning for Life*. St. Louis: Concordia Publishing House, 1997.

Heiges, Donald R. *The Christian's Calling*. Philadelphia: Fortress Press, 1958.

Hill, Jonathan. *The History of Christian Thought*. Downers Grove, Ill: Intervarsity Press, 2003.

Jahsmann, J.H. *What's Lutheran in Education?* St. Louis: Concordia Publishing House, 1960.

Janzow, W. Theophil, editor. *Perspectives on Ministry*. River Forest, Ill: Lutheran Education Association, 1981.

Koberle, Adolf. *The Quest for Holiness*. Minneapolis: Augsburg Publishing House, 1936 (reprinted in the Concordia Heritage Series, Concordia Publishing House).

Koehneke, D. R. "The Call Into the Holy Ministry." In T. Laetsch (editor), *The Abiding Word*. St. Louis: Concordia Publishing House, 1946.

Kolb, Robert. *The Christian Faith: A Lutheran Exposition*. St. Louis: Concordia Publishing House, 1993.

Moser, Carl, editor. *The Call of a Lutheran Educator*. St. Louis: Concordia Publishing House, 1994 (Bulletin #S08700).

McKechnie, P. *The First Christian Centuries: Perspectives on the Early Church*. Downers Grove, Ill: Intervarsity Press, 2001.

Mueller, Arnold C. *The Ministry of the Lutheran Teacher: A Study to Determine the Position of the Lutheran Parish School Teacher Within the Public Ministry of the Church*. St. Louis: Concordia Publishing House, 1964.

Oberman, Heiko A. *Luther: Man Between God and the Devil*. New York: Image Doubleday, 1992.

Ozment, Steven. *Protestants: The Birth of a Revolution*. New York: Doubleday, 1991.

Painter, F.V.N. *Luther on Education*. St. Louis: Concordia Publishing House, 1965.

Parker, T. H. L. *Calvin: An Introduction to His Thought*. Louisville, Kentucky: Westminster John Knox Press, 1995.

Pragman, James H. *Traditions of Ministry: A History of the Doctrine of the Ministry in Lutheran Theology*. St. Louis: Concordia Publishing House, 1983.

Rietschel, William C. *An Introduction to the Foundations of Lutheran Education*. St. Louis: Concordia Academic Press, 2000.

Schmidt, Stephen A. *Powerless Pedagogues: An Interpretive Essay on the History of the Lutheran Teacher in the Missouri Synod*. River Forest, Ill: Lutheran Education Association, 1972.

Shelley, Bruce L. *Church History in Plain Language*. Dallas: Word, 1982.

Simmons, Ernest L. *Lutheran Higher Education: An Introduction*. Minneapolis: Augsburg Fortress, 1998.

Stellhorn, August C. *Schools of the Lutheran Church–Missouri Synod*. St. Louis: Concordia Publishing House, 1963.

Veith, Gene E. *The Spirituality of the Cross*. St. Louis: Concordia Publishing House, 1999.

Walther, C. F. W. *The True Visible Church and The Form of a Christian Congregation*. St. Louis: Concordia Publishing House, 1961.

———. *Church and Ministry: Witnesses of the Evangelical Lutheran Church on the Question of the Church and the Ministry*. St. Louis: Concordia Publishing House, 1987.

Wingren, Gustaf. *Luther on Vocation*. Philadelphia: Muhlenberg Press, 1957 (reprinted in the Concordia Heritage Series, Concordia Publishing House).

Index

L

labor model, 138, 144
laity, 63
Law and Gospel, 13, 32, 33, 57, 75,
    101, 112
leadership, 143
Lewin, Kurt, 133
Lewis, C. S., 133
Luther, 31, 33, 40, 61, 98, 112
Lutheran Confessions, 89, 90, 112,
    114

M

makarios, 131
ministry, 60, 69, 71
Moses, 124

N

Nafzger, Samuel, 61, 99

O

office, 91
offices and titles, 141
oikonomia, 119
Origen, 137, 147

P

passion, 123
Paul, 3, 5, 16, 20, 21, 23, 29, 35,
    36, 38, 46, 49, 50, 51, 52,
    53, 55, 64, 66, 70, 84, 85,
    86, 87, 90, 91, 96, 98, 100,
    102, 103, 105, 110, 112,
    114, 116, 118, 119, 132
policy-based governance, 143
priesthood of all believers, 61, 75,
    88, 128, 145
prophet, 87
public education, 7, 37, 140
public ministry, 43, 45, 86, 88, 89,
    91, 130, 145

R

Reformation, 41
righteousness, 102

S

sabbath year, 49
scholasticism, 40
signs, 118, 124
simul iustus et peccator, 102
sin, 32, 102, 117
sola fide, 99
sola scriptura, 99
spiritual gifts, 75
Spitz, L. W., 61
still, small voice, 117

T

teacher of the church
    qualities, ix, 5, 12
    who is?, 2
teaching,
    and women, 16
    as action, 21, 55
    biblical content, 19
    biblical words, 15, 81
    in Acts, 83
    in Jesus' ministry, 81
    in Paul's ministry, 52
    in public schools, 22, 27
    in Scripture, 15, 79, 81
tension, 32, 34, 45, 54, 91
theological traditions, 30, 89, 93,
    95
theology of glory, 103
theology of the cross, 103
titles, 141
two kingdom doctrine, 30, 31, 43,
    45, 47, 105, 140
two strategies, 31, 43, 45, 47

U

University of Wittenberg, 40

V

vocation, 12, 72, 106

W

Walther, C. F. W., 21, 51
will, 104
    bondage of the will, 101
    free will, 101
    God's will, 109, 111, 114
Wingren, Gustaf, 113
Word as external, 144
world, 32
    five current conditions, 6
worship, 76